Elsie May Dearest

A Collection of Letters from 1918 to 1945

A snapshot of life in a bygone era

Compiled and edited by Sally Prytherch

ISBN: 978-1-910181-48-5

Printed and published by Anchorprint Group Ltd
January 2018

Many thanks to Tony Hartell, Linda Storer, Christine Uzzel, Timothy Hartell, Jackie Harris, Nicholas Hartell, John Lane, Nigel Lane, and David Lane for your co-operation.

sal.cherith@ntlworld.com

Contents

This book is dedicated to Elsie and Harold's great, great grandchildren:

Martha Rose
Elsie Eira Mai
Albert Arthur
Sophia Jane

Danny Isaac
Louie James
Theo Stanley
Phoebe Belle
Freddie Hausmann
Ruby Mae
Nancy Florence

Cameron (by marriage)
Elsie Maria (by marriage)

It is also dedicated to any future great, great grandchildren of Elsie and Harold whose names can be hand written above into copies of this book.
It is hoped that they, their parents, their children, and their children's children may treasure this snapshot of life in another age gifted to them by Elsie, Harold and Cyril.

And to Elsie and Harold's children:

My lovely Uncle Tony Hartell, whose help and encouragement with this project has been invaluable.

And in memory of:

My equally lovely Dad, Peter Hartell (26.4.1928 – 30.1.2013)

Pamela Lane, Elsie and Harold's daughter
(11.7.1926 – 17.10.1986)

Forward by Tony Hartell

The following are random memories of my mother, Elsie May Pamphilon (formerly Hartell), nee Martin, during the years from the 1930s to the 1950s, spanning my childhood and youth.

These memories have been prompted by the research carried out by my niece Sally Prytherch, the author of a social history woven around Elsie and Newtown Linford, Leicestershire, a beautiful English village.

I hope that these notes may, in some small way, compliment the author's extensive and painstaking research.

My parents, Harold and Elsie, built a large semi-bungalow on three-quarters of an acre of land in the village of Newtown Linford during the 1930s. It overlooked Bradgate Park, some 1060 acres of natural parkland bequeathed by Charles Bennion in 1928 to the people of Leicestershire in perpetuity. Elsie was undoubtedly the driving force to move out of Leicester as she was determined that her three children Pamela (12), Harold known as 'Pete' (10) and I, Tony (8) should grow up in a healthy environment.

The park was, of course, a perfect playground and we made good use of it. Life was good and, from a child's point of view, idyllic. I relate this only to emphasize the magnitude of the impending disaster. Our father died from a cerebral haemorrhage in July 1938.

Overnight, Elsie found herself a widow with three young children and an income of one guinea (twenty-one shillings) a week. After a tragically short time as a happy, and contented wife and mother, her grief at our father's death was indescribable, compounded by poverty staring her in the face.

War with Germany was declared in September 1939, and though this brought no immediate danger to us, there were further pressures such as food and petrol rationing, clothing coupons, the blackout, air raid precautions, gas masks, etc, all of which bore down on her.

Eventually, and inevitably, the decision was forced on her to formally open up her dearly beloved home as a guest house. A comparatively small alteration was made upstairs to form two additional bedrooms, a large sign was erected announcing that the house was RAC (Royal Automobile Association) recommended and suddenly there were strangers in the house. Some were friendly, others withdrawn, often seeking respite from bombing (of Coventry and elsewhere). Others used their precious holidays from dangerous work in munitions factories or simply to recover from exhausting long hours on vital war work.

The work involved in running the Guest House fell mainly on my mother and sister, with some part-time help by a lady from a nearby village. In addition to the obvious work of cooking, cleaning, shopping and attending to the needs of the guests, there was the very considerable burden of red tape required by the Ministry of Food in connection with the supply of meals to feed the guests. Ingredients were very restricted and The Ministry offered recipes using such foodstuffs that were seasonally available and I remember, with distaste, the dreaded steamed tomato pudding which, when opened, collapsed in a gory puddle to cries of disgust. I know that the administrative work caused my mother considerable stress. The penalties for false or inaccurate returns were draconian.

In 1945 my sister Pamela was 'called up' to do work of national importance and she elected to join the Women's Land Army. She had been a tower of strength to my mother and this development was yet another blow, and clearly stretched Elsie's indomitable courage almost to breaking point.

There lived in the village, just across the road, a lady called Marion Richardson (1) who had been a friend to my mother since we moved to Newtown and it was at this time that she proved what a true friend she was, spending long hours talking to and encouraging my mother, and I know that Mum would be delighted that after all these years, Marion's faithful friendship, support and unfailing good humour was acknowledged. Marion's Cottage, now the Bradgate Park information shop, was named after her.

After a number of years struggling on her own to run the Guest House and bring up three children, my mother married a former family friend Cyril Pamphilon in 1941. They had corresponded for some time while he was being treated for TB at nearby Markfield Sanatorium. He completed his recuperation as a resident at the Guest House.

I feel blessed that my mother was a woman of such great courage and determination who took all that life threw at her, fought her way through and lived to the ripe old age of 98. I am immensely proud and privileged to have been her son.

Tony Hartell

Introduction
By Sally Prytherch (nee Hartell) daughter of Peter Hartell

After Elsie May Pamphilon died in July 1997 a 'roll top desk' went to live in her son Peter's office at his home until 2013. Unknown to anyone but Peter, within it were a series of letters dating from 1918 through to 1945 written from Elsie's first husband, Harold Hartell, and her second husband, Cyril Pamphilon. It is from these letters and a short journal by Elsie that this book has written itself giving a fascinating insight into the lives of ordinary, yet extraordinary, people at that time.

Although I never knew my grandfather I feel that I have come to know him, and Cyril, very well through the letters. These combined with Elsie's journal have given much more of an insight into the life of my grandmother.

Now in my fifty-eighth year, images, memories and sensations flood back of happy carefree days staying with Grandma and Grandpa Pamphilon at their bungalow overlooking the reservoir at Thornton in Leicestershire. Black treacle on my porridge; the warmth of under floor heating on the soles of my feet; the unique smell in the hallway of lavender, old furniture and polish, tinged with a hint of cucumber soaked in vinegar. Mashed up red salmon covered with melted butter and re-set in a little dish, spread onto bread for tea; bread and semi-crystallized honey; the unique smell and taste of quince jelly; round, flat Quality Street toffees and long cigar-shaped chocolate covered toffees which sat on the mantelpiece above the fireplace in an oblong brass or copper dish with rounded corners. The toffees were always offered before we left and had to be wrestled into submission between our teeth because they were far too large and awkward to fit into our four and five-year-old mouths. Running in the garden which sloped down toward the reservoir with my two sisters and brother; long walks with Grandma and my little sister, Linda, around the reservoir, picking posies of yellow primroses in the spring; pleasures not availed to children of today because of wildlife and plant conservation.

Reflecting on these things evoked other memories of being taken at four and a half years old to see Mary Poppins at the cinema, (released December 23rd 1964), with my cousin John. The memory of feeling very afraid when Grandma left us while she went to buy ice-cream in the interval is strong – followed by feelings of immense relief on her return. Other memories of Grandma's oil paintings created by her own hand, adorning the walls of her bungalow; Shakespeare, Little Women, Water Babies, poetry books and other classics bought for birthday and Christmas presents having special magic about them because they were from Grandma, who loved books and passed that love on to me. The pale blue Ford Anglia that she would drive us around in when we stayed with her. The respect we had for this formidable yet kindly little woman with a big personality who was always interested in our school work and academic achievements. Listening to stories Grandma had written for broadcasting on the BBC radio, sitting close to the very large, old tape recorder and watching intensely as the huge spools of tape rolled from one side of the machine to the other. Her relentless campaigning to stop fluoride being added to drinking water because she believed it would be harmful to children rather than beneficial. Special thick baby orange juice that glooped out of the bottle, enriched with vitamins and only ever consumed at Grandma's house. The heated, but friendly, opinionated debates she would have with my father which completely went over my childish head but left me feeling slightly uncomfortable.

These are memories which link the present with the past. The information and memories within the letters in this book reach back into the lives of my father, uncle, aunt and grandparents and give an insight into their lives at that time. Through these letters compiled in book form, there is also a sense of Harold, Elsie and Cyril reaching forward into the lives of my own children, grandchildren, future great grandchildren, nieces, nephews, great nieces and great nephews and anyone interested enough to delve into the treasure held between these pages.

Harold writes about everyday life, there is a description of his trip to the Isle of Wight to see the Schneider Trophy event, lots of references to food and everyday things like Bovril, the silent movies, his first experience of a 'talkie' movie and seaside holidays. He makes reference to journeys from Leicester Railway Station. He also writes from a convalescent home in Southport near Liverpool, a trip possibly funded by the Co-op in Leicester, where he worked as a clerk for many years. He talks about the daily salt baths that were part of his treatment, the food, and the other noisy patients. His loneliness when he is parted from his wife, and his love and concern for her and his children comes through strongly.

After his untimely death on July 3rd 1938, at age 42, Harold was buried in Newtown Linford church yard in Leicestershire. His unusual headstone in the form of a birdbath is still there. Elsie fought the local authorities of the day for permission to have the memorial erected, a testament to her tenacity and determination.

In 1940, Cyril's letters take up similar themes. Many are written from Markfield Sanatorium, where he was being treated for tuberculosis (TB), and there is more of an insight into the Theosophical Society to which they belonged. Elsie had by that time turned her and Harold's dream home, just outside Bradgate Park into a guesthouse.

As well as her journal, Elsie was the author of a booklet about Lady Jane Grey and Bradgate Park. A later version of her publication is included in this book. Peter and Tony, her sons, had to sell the publication outside the park gates when times were hard, along with homemade lemonade.

The original plan for Harold and Cyril's letters was to type them up just for immediate family, but from a social and local history perspective it seemed a shame, even a crime, not to share the story. It is so much more than just a factual document; it is an insight into their physical, emotional, and everyday lives at that time, and so the process began.........

This is the story of Elsie May Martin, Harold Hartell and Cyril Pamphilon as well as the friends and relatives who touched their lives. The creation of this book has been a moving, fascinating, enthralling journey and I hope will be enjoyed by all who turn these pages. I hope Grandma would approve. As an avid writer herself I am sure that she would.

In the words of T.S Eliot:

"Time past and time present are both perhaps present in time future"

From: Four Quartets (Burnt Norton) by T.S Elliot.
(Licence to print granted by kind permission of Faber and Faber Ltd, publishers)

The additional supporting information has been gleaned from the memories of Anthony Hartell (Tony), Carol Hartell the wife of Harold (Peter) Hartell, Jim Martin, Hazel Allan, Alma Tingay, Shirley Raithby, other relatives and sources named in the acknowledgements, bibliography and from family tree research.

Part 1

Family History the Historical and Geographical Context

Chapter 1

Newfoundpool and Elsie's Family

Newfoundpool, known as 'The Pool' in Leicester, is where Elsie May Martin was born to Emma Sarah and Henry Martin in 1899. It is where her family lived, where she and Harold Hartell shared a house with Harold's aunt and uncle in the early days of their marriage, and where their story begins.

There is evidence that Newfoundpool may have originally been linked to The Augustinian Friary in Leicester (www.british-history.ac.uk). Entrepreneur, Isaac Harrison in the 1830's is thought to have owned the land on which Newfoundpool is located. He had hoped to profit from a natural spring by turning it into a spa, and a house was built where locals could bathe in the medicinal water. Countryside originally surrounded the area and although initially popular, the venture only lasted for four or five years (Stevens 2014).

'The Pool' is spoken of fondly by Jim Martin, Henry Martin's grandson by his son Joel. Joel was Elsie's younger half brother and 'The Pool' was the community that Elsie and her siblings would have known while in Leicester. The terraced streets are still inter-connected by narrow (now gated) alleyways or 'jittys'. It is easy to imagine children of another era scampering up and down these shortcuts on hearing their mothers summon them to come in for tea; or to see them in the mind's eye playing hide and seek or crouching invisibly in an alley to avoid a thrashing for some misdemeanor. These 'jitty's' with a little imagination give a real visual insight into community life of long ago. 'Newfoundpool Working Men's Club and Institute' at 55 Beatrice Road was frequented by Joel, and the club is still very much part of the community life today. Jim remembers 'The Pool' being fully self-contained with coal merchants, bakers, butchers and greengrocers all contributing to the life and economy of the community.

On the 1904 Godfrey's Ordnance Survey map looking from west to east the first street at the top of 'The Pool' is Ingle Street. Nook Street or 'The Nook', made up of only a few houses, is a little connecting road to Hawthorne Street. These are followed by Alma Street, Rowan Street, Ruby Street, Ivanhoe Street, Sylvan Street, Oban Street and Newport Street. The combined first letters of each, with the exception of Nook Street, spells out I. HARRISON. At the bottom end of 'The Pool' Saint Augustine's Church (now demolished) was situated between Newport Street and Fosse Road North. Longitudinally, either side, the streets are framed by Pool Road on one side and Beatrice Road on the other. Elsie and her family lived in Hawthorne Street, Nook Street, Ingle Street, and Pool Road. Joel later lived in Alma Street as an adult. Elsie and Harold sometime after 1921, moved half a mile out of Newfoundpool from Pool Road to their own family home on St Pauls Road, a small cul-de-sac off Wentworth Road. This overlooked Fosse Road Recreation Ground close to Fosse Road North. Between 1921 and 1929 before coming back to 'The Pool' they had lived for a short time at Scaptoft, a district of Leicester.

One of the puzzling things about the family history of those who lived in 'The Pool' at the beginning of the century was how often they moved house, sometimes moving just a street or two away. During a walk through 'The Pool' with Jim Martin, the conclusion was reached that they probably moved through circumstances, as rooms within the houses would mostly have been rented out with more than one family living in each home. Perhaps frequent moves were required for a larger bedroom or more space to accommodate the ever increasing numbers of children being born, or for a more affordable rent. Jim, on setting out to buy his own house in the late 1950's recalls his father Joel stating that "A working man doesn't buy his own house!" and that mortgages were "a millstone around your neck" and should be avoided by the working classes.

Elsie May Martin was born at 21 Hawthorne Street, Newfoundpool on May 5th 1899. Eighteen months later her brother, **Henry** also known as Harry, was born on November 28**th** 1900, followed by a sister **Ethel Maud** on January 5**th** 1903. Their youngest sibling **Emma** was born on July 26**th** 1904 at Ingle Street, Newfoundpool. Tragically, their mother Emma Sarah died on July 30th 1904 aged almost 25, four days after giving birth to baby Emma. Elsie was 5 years old, Henry was 3 and Ethel was only 18 months old when they lost their mother.

Henry, who was present at his wife's death, was left with four small children to bring up alone. At 4 days old baby Emma was handed to Sarah Hobbs the unofficial nurse and midwife present at the delivery. She and her husband Harry originally from Northampton lived at 150 Pool Road, just a couple of streets away from Ingle Street and Sarah became baby Emma's 'wet-nurse'. Emma was brought up by Harry and Sarah Hobbs with their own family and an adopted son David Barratt. Although the Hobbs were poor Emma was loved and very happy. In the 1911 census aged 6, she was described as 'the adopted child' of Harry and Sarah Hobbs.

After their mother's death in 1904, Elsie, Henry, and Ethel were sent to live at the home of their paternal grandparents at The Blackbirds Inn, Flitwick in Bedfordshire. Joel Martin, their grandfather, a carpenter and publican had died in 1901 and Mary Ann their grandmother had continued to run the public house. Fred Martin, Henry's older brother became the proprietor of the Blackbirds. He is pictured outside the pub on an old photograph. Fred was also Clerk of Works for a time at the Princes Essoldo Cinema in Granby Street Leicester. 'Pictures' had been shown there since 1898 when it was the Temperance Hall.

Emma had only had one unhappy trip to the Bedfordshire countryside to visit her siblings. She was chased by geese and never wanted to repeat the visit again. Sarah Hobbs encouraged Emma to accept the yearly invitations to spend Christmas Day with her biological family at her father's home at 227 Beatrice Road, Leicester. Emma would stay for a short a time as possible much preferring to be at home with the Hobbs at 150 Pool Road.

It was probably around the time of their grandmother Mary Ann's death in 1909 that Elsie, Henry and Ethel returned to Leicester to live permanently with Henry their father and **Evelyn (nee Aldwinkle)** his second wife, who he had married in September 1905. After the death of his first wife, Henry had gone to the Leicester Workhouse to find someone to look after his children. Evelyn already had a son Sidney who was 8 months old when she married Henry.

In the summer of 1915 when Evelyn would have been four months pregnant with her youngest son George, another tragedy struck the Martin household. Henry, Elsie's brother was aged 14, and had a job as a grocer's errand boy. He was said to be a studious, good looking boy with curly red hair. Many family members have told the story of how he fell asleep in a glass summer house or greenhouse and died of sunstroke at the family home in Beatrice Road. One family myth which may or may not be true was that he was reading when he fell asleep.

Young Henry died on June 16th 1915 and his death certificate states the cause of death as 'meningitis' followed by two letters that resemble T.B. In 1915 tuberculosis (TB) was a common problem with cases of TB meningitis being much more prevalent then. The infection occurs when TB is present somewhere else in the body, usually the lungs, and then spreads to the brain. TB in the lungs can lie dormant for several months before manifesting as an infection. The symptoms of meningitis and sunstroke are quite similar, muscle aches, fever, headaches, dizziness, nausea and vomiting and could have been initially confused (Meningitisnow 2017). The complete story of Henry's death will never be known, but it remains a tragedy and would have affected the family greatly. Emma, his younger sister, was said to have been extremely fond of him and as they were quite close in age probably attended Ingle Street School together. It is thought that Emma may have had some input into his learning to read, as she had with David Barratt / Hobbs to who she was as close as a brother.

Emma had very little contact with her father and stepmother and resisted all attempts by Henry to reclaim her by offering her a home with him when she was 14, feeling that he only wanted her when she became old enough to earn a wage. Henry disowned her when she refused to return home and told her siblings to sever contact with her as well. Emma never got over her brother's death and named one of her own sons Harry as he resembled Henry (Harry). They both had red hair.

Henry and Evelyn had seven children of their own with only four surviving into adulthood. The children were all brought up at 227 Beatrice Road, Newfoundpool, Leicester. Elsie was known to have disliked Evelyn and always felt that her father had married beneath him. Harold's early letters suggest some discord between Elsie and her father.

Henry served with the Royal Engineers in the 'Special Brigade' and 'Explosive Division' in France during the 1914-1918 War. After the First World War he worked as a bricklayer or a builder's labourer. He had a reputation for having a hot temper even in his younger days which he retained in later life. He was known to have had drinking bouts and his family often wondered if this was due to the way he had been affected by his wartime experiences. Henry died on August 12th 1944 aged 69 at Hillcrest Hospital, the former workhouse, from 'cerebral degeneration, arterial sclerosis and myocarditis'. Evelyn outlived Henry by 11 years and also died at the The Hillcrest Hospital probably where her life with Henry had begun.

Ethel's daughter Joan is mentioned in Cyril's letters in the 1940's as helping out at Elsie's guesthouse with cooking and cleaning.

Elsie in her later years often told people that she was one of three sisters all with the initials E.M. It is unknown where and when she and Harold Hartell met, but they certainly lived within the same geographical area of Newfoundpool in Leicester and were corresponding in 1918 when she was 18 years old.

(Appendix B at the back of the book gives a more detailed family history)

Elsie's Family Tree

Elsie in her late teens or early 20's

Elsie's Family Tree – fold out

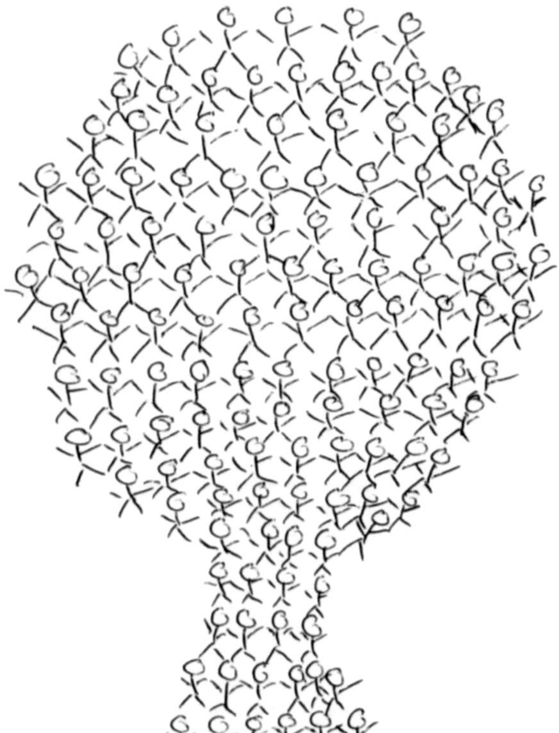

Elsie's family photographs

Paternal grandfather

Joel Martin (1837-1901)
Publican at the Blackbirds Inn,
Flitwick,
Bedfordshire

Paternal grandmother

Mary Ann Martin (1839-1909)

Mary Ann Martin also known as Margaret was Joel's wife. Together they ran The Blackbirds Inn for 18 years

Elsie's parents, siblings and relatives

Above Left: Elsie's mother, Emma Sarah Martin (nee Joyce) (1879-1904). Right: Elsie's father, Henry Martin (1875-1944). The photograph set in a brooch belonged to Elsie; a photograph of Harold was on the reverse side.

Above: Fred and Mrs Martin, Henry's brother outside 'The Blackbirds', Flitwick

Left: Elsie May Martin
(1899-1997)
aged about two years old.

Right: Elsie in her teens

Above: Henry (Harry) Martin (1900-1915) died in the greenhouse at 14 years old

Ethel Maud Martin
(1903-1979)

Left: Emma Martin, Dave Barratt (also fostered and adopted by the Hobbs), and Sarah Hobbs

Right: Harry Hobbs

Emma Martin (1904-1986)

Henry and Evelyn's Family

Front from left: Joel Martin, Henry and Evelyn Martin (nee Aldwinkle), George Martin (Georgie) on Evelyn's knee. Middle: behind Joel is James Harold, middle between Henry and Evelyn is Florence Evelyn (Eva). Back from left: Ethel Maud Martin, Elsie May Martin, Emma Martin and Sidney Aldwinkle

Left: Florence Evelyn Martin (Eva) as a toddler

Henry and Evelyn Martin

Above and right: Henry Martin at 227 Beatrice Road, Newfoundpool

Left: Henry Martin with grandchild Jimmy and right: Evelyn with Jimmy at 227 Beatrice Road, Newfoundpool.

Left: Joel Martin (1910-1976) Henry and Evelyn's son (Elsie's half brother), with his daughter Evelyn taken in the back yard at Alma Street, Newfoundpool.

Chapter 2
Harold's Family

Harold's mother **Edith (nee Owen)** (1876-1939) was born in Bristol, and her father, a leather currier originated from Carmarthenshire in Wales. **George Hartell** (1876-1918) Harold's father and his family came from Staffordshire. They were shoe finishers and lived in Leicester before moving to Avins Yard, Long Street, Atherstone, Warwickshire, where George and Edith lived with George's parents for a period of time.

Edith and George married in September 1895 at Leicester. George earned a living as a shoe finisher and Edith was a cigar maker. After they married they initially lived with Edith's maternal grandparents **James** and **Harriet Hall (nee Knight)** at 14 Burgess Road in Leicester. **Harold**, Edith's first child was born on November 20th 1895. In total Harold's parents had 12 children, and seven of them died in infancy (see Appendix C).

Two years after Harold was born Edith gave birth to a son **George** on 26**th** November 1897. In the 1901 census when George was 3 years old he was living with his paternal grandparents, **Elizabeth** and **George Hartell**, in Atherstone, and Harold was still living in Leicester with his great-grandparents James and Harriet Hall. Fourteen months after George's birth Edith had a daughter, who they also named **Edith**. In May 1900 another son, **Horace** was born, but sadly he died aged only 11 months old from pertussis (whooping cough), pneumonia and convulsions. Horace's illness may explain why 3 year old George had been sent to live with his paternal grandparents, and why Harold aged 5 years old remained with his maternal great-grandparents at Burgess Road, Leicester. Edith their sister, however, had continued to live with her parents in Leicester and later in Atherstone. In her adult life Edith and was known to be a kind and charitable woman with 'a heart of gold'.

On May 16TH 1907 young George aged 9 was admitted to the Desford Industrial School, a reform institution, for being 'out of control'. His grandmother Elizabeth had died on February 8th 1902 when he was 5 years old and it is likely that he was sent back to Leicester to live with his family. By 1911 the rest of the family except for Harold had moved to Avins Yard, Atherstone.

Avins Yard was the 158th of at least 164 yards. They were all built mostly in the back yards of the houses on Long Street, the main road that still runs through Atherstone and became known as 'The Yards'. The houses in Avins Yard were built hurriedly and were not well constructed. They were added to during the eighteenth century and were mostly rented cottages (Friends of Atherstone Heritage 2012). The houses had no foundations and were built onto bare earth with red brick quarry tile floors covered with linoleum or a rag rug. The dividing walls were only one brick in thickness (Alcock 2008). Each house was approximately 4 metres by 4 metres with 2 rooms, one up and one down, and built back to back with only one window at the front of the house. Each yard shared a water pump, one or two 'privies' cleaned out nightly by the 'soil men', an ash pit, and an open drain which ran down the middle of the yard (Friends of Atherstone Heritage 2012)(Dirveiks L. Vero J.). In 1911 a health report was carried out by a Dr. Herring on the living conditions of the Atherstone Yards citing high incidences of TB, infectious diseases such as scarlet fever, and high infant mortality. The report recommended demolition of 'The Yards' but Avins Yard was not demolished until 25 years later in 1936 (Friends of Atherstone Heritage 2012). The entry to Avins Yard from Long Street would have originally been situated at the Station Road end of the Street, not far from the railway station and can still be seen there today.

During their time in Atherstone the family would have no doubt witnessed, or even taken part in the annual 'Atherstone Ball Game' which has been played on Long Street by the men of the town on Shrove Tuesday for 800 years (Appendix C).

Harold was aged 15 in 1911 and living with his maternal grandparents **John and Elizabeth Owen (nee Hall)** at 1 Court A Craven Street, Leicester. He worked as a clerk, probably at the Co-op bakery where, except for his time in the Army, he spent most of his working life. He was still with his grandparents at the same address 6 years later in 1917.

In 1912, aged 15 years George had left the Desford Industrial School and joined the Army as a musician having played the cornet in the school band for four years. As he was too young for military service his rank was 'Boy' and he was initially with the Training Reserve before being transferred to India with the 2nd Leicestershire Battalion. He joined the Duke of Wellington's West Riding Regiment and was killed in action in Flanders, France on 20**th** September 1917 at the Menin Road Ridge Battle five years after joining the Army. This was the first day of the second phase of the Third Battle of Ypres. Thousands of men were killed at Ypres or drowned in the quagmire of mud in appalling conditions. Frank Hurley an Australian photographer on the front line reported in 1917 '*...for there is no place in eternity that is more hellish'.* George is remembered on the regimental memorial stone the Tyne Cot Memorial, Zonnebeke, Belgium. His name is also on a memorial stone of Swithland slate at the old Desford School at the end of an avenue of horse chestnut trees as well as being written in the Golden Roll of Honour book at Leicester Cathedral (Appendix C).

On September 8th 1914, George, Harold's father, had enlisted in The Royal Warwickshire Regiment. He was discharged from the Army on 12**th** December 1917, after receiving a penetrating gunshot wound to the head and was brought back to Leicester. He died a year later on December 22**nd** 1918 aged 42, from a cerebral abscess caused by his injuries. All the regiments to which he belonged fought in the Third Battle of Ypres and it is likely he was wounded in Phase 3 from 26th October to 10th November. It is very likely that he fought in some of the same battles as his son George. His memorial can be seen in Welford Road Cemetery, Leicester.

Edith's two youngest children, **Frank** born in 1917 and **Doris** in 1918 died within weeks of their births, Frank from gastro enteritis, and Doris from 'marasmus' and both are buried at Welford Road Cemetery, Leicester. Marasmus can be linked with influenza, premature birth, and malnutrition (Reid 2005) and in 1918 and 1919 the world was in the grip of the Spanish influenza pandemic. Between 1895 and 1917 Edith had given birth to 12 children, 7 of them died in infancy. Her youngest surviving child Walter was born in September 1915 (Appendix C).

The period between 1890 and 1910 when Edith and George were raising their family had a very high infant mortality rate in Leicester. Infants were often left with unsuitable minders while their mothers had to work. Many infants died from gastro enteritis and diarrhoea. Even very young babies were fed inappropriate diets of condensed milk, cow's milk or liquid pulps made up of sago, oatmeal and arrowroot or 'pap' made from bread and water which were detrimental rather than beneficial to them nutritionally. Overcrowded living conditions, inadequate housing and poor sanitation and hygiene would have increased incidences of infection, as well as respiratory conditions linked with measles and whooping cough (Amos 2012).

In 1948 Elsie May, then Pamphilon, wrote an article for 'The Socialist Leader' entitled 'The Good Old Days? Past and Present'. It described the working conditions around the time that she and Harold were young when their parents would have been struggling to bring up their families. She began, *"In the so called 'good old days' just prior to the 1914 – 1918 war, I stayed for a period with friends who kept a grocery shop, in a working class district, in a Midlands town, noted for the manufacture of boots, shoes and hosiery."* Elsie went on to describe how trade was very bad with factory hands working only 6 months of the year which created the need for women to work as well. They would often stay at home for only one month with their new born babies before going out to work. Children under school age were looked after by 'nurse-women' who were often outside workers for the factories as well as child carers. Pay for 'kid-minding' as it was called was poor, so the 'nurse-women' undertook work for the factories, *"toeing socks, and solutioning and machining insides to the outsides of the uppers of boots and shoes, the pungent smell of the solution used permeating the clothes and house of the operator. The pay for this work was fairly good but had to be fetched from the factory and returned when finished. One child would be taken with the 'nurse-woman' in a perambulator, with the work piled up around it, but other children in the woman's care would be dosed with a little laudanum to make them sleep until she returned".* The town described could very well have been Leicester, known for the hosiery and boot and shoe trade, especially as it didn't regain the status of 'City' until 1919 (Beckett 2006).

Edith was living at 48 Merridale Road, Leicester at the time of her husband George's death from his war injuries in December 1918. She had already lost 7 children as infants, was present at the deaths of them all and had lost her son George in The Great War. Only 5 of her children had continued into adulthood and 4 had families of their own. Edith died on June 14th 1939 when she was 62 years old. Her home address was still 48 Merridale Road Leicester, and she died in the Towers Hospital Leicester from peritonitis and a perforating ulcer.

Harold grew up with his great-grandparents and grandparents and probably did not know his parents and siblings very well. His own children had no knowledge of his siblings and his sister Edith's family had no knowledge of Harold or George.

Harold and Elsie tell the rest of their own story through the letters that follow and Elsie's journal.

(Appendix C at the back of the book gives a more detailed family history).

Harold's Family Tree

Edith

Above: Harold's sister Edith (1899-1963) who 'had a heart of gold'

Harold's Family Tree – fold out

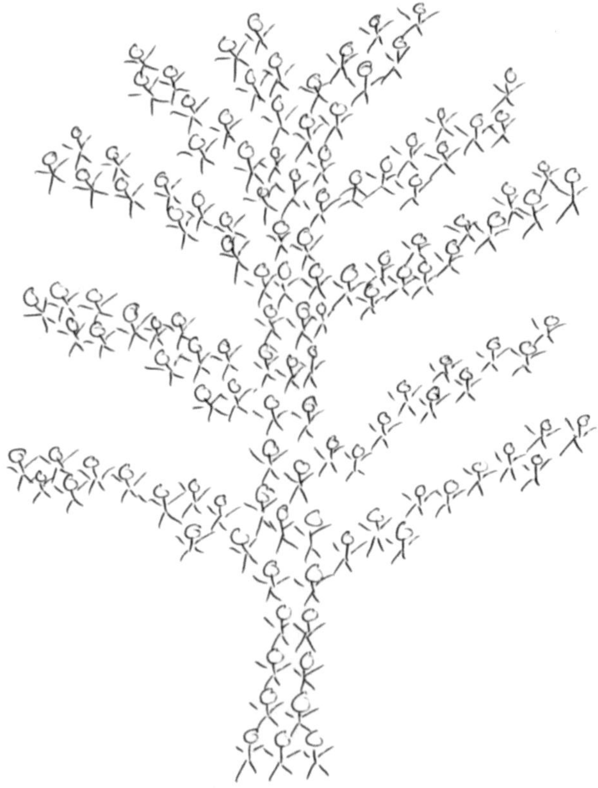

Atherstone

Above: Avins Yard Atherstone looking toward Long Street.
Below: looking toward the Station Street end (around 1910)

Above: Long Street, Atherstone with workhouse in the early 1900s

The above mural was commissioned by Christine Freeman (Jenking) local author and painted by Michael Chetwynd from Baddesley Ensor. It shows the Railway Station, Vero and Everitt's hat factory and the Atherstone Ball Game in progress. The original beautiful colour painting is at Bracebridge Court Care Home. Christine Freeman holds the copyright.

Part 2

Letters to Elsie from Harold 1918 – 1938

Chapter 3
Romance with a Soldier

For a period during the 1914-1918 war Harold served with the Cameronian Scottish Rifles Regiment (2) indicated by his cap badge and photograph. His first letters to Elsie were written from Witham, in Essex in 1918 where he was stationed. There does not appear to be any record of Harold's military service possibly because many WW1 records were destroyed in September 1940 during a German bomb attack on London (www.nationalarchives.gov.uk). Harold's first letter to Elsie may indicate that he had signed up until 1920. There is a hint that he had a medical problem in 1918, and the letters imply that he might not have been eligible for transfer, so he may have remained at Witham (see letter 12.7.1918). What is clear is that he and Elsie were romantically involved and were very unhappy to be separated at that time. Family history suggests that Elsie ran away from home to marry Harold. They married on November 23rd 1918 in the parish church at Witham, Braintree in Essex. Harold was a soldier and Elsie's profession on their marriage certificate is 'munitionette'. Their marriage certificate also states that Elsie was 21 years old, when she was in fact 18, and Harold was 23. Parental permission was normally required at that time to marry if under the age of 21 and from Harold's letters it would appear that her father may not have been happy about their intention to marry. The early letters give an impression of discord with Henry, although Elsie spoke fondly of him in later life. Harold was a quiet and softly spoken man with a 'droll' sense of humour which comes through in his letters.

(Punctuation within the following letters has been added or adjusted to enhance the readability of the text)

(R.E. Regimental Engineering Store
or Royal Engineering Store)
Harold Hartell
R.E. Main Store
Witham
4/5/1918

My darling Sweetheart
Just a line to wish you very many happy returns of the day. That two years hence may see you happy and contented is my dearest wish and hope. But cheer up darling, time will soon fly by, and we shall not always be parted. I only wish I could be with you today to help make your happiness complete. With every best wish for your health and happiness and best and fondest love,
From your ever loving sweetheart
Harold
XXXXXXX
XXXXXXX
XXXXX

Harold Hartell
R.E. Main Store
Witham
12/7/1918
Friday

My own dear sweetheart
Just a few lines in answer to your loving and ever so welcome letter which I have just received (dinner time) and to thank you very much for the cigarettes. I have been wondering why you hadn't written lately, but now I know that you were not fit to write. To tell you the truth, I shouldn't have been a little bit surprised to see you walking down Maldon Rd any day. Darling, I am ever so sorry to learn that you have been so queer just lately. I certainly think you are acting wisely by coming down, because I do think that if you don't soon

have a change from Leicester, you will be having another breakdown and you know full well that I wouldn't have that happen for worlds. Sweetheart, I am very sorry to hear that you have had another nasty letter from your dada, I am sure I don't know what really is the best thing to do but I do know that I shouldn't have a quarter as patience with him as you have. My sweetheart, I know how very hard it is to forget these things, but try your hardest during the next few days not to brood over it, and when you get down here I will try my best to make you forget these unhappy things. Dearest, you will have had my letter by now telling you all about the Medical board. I think when you get that letter it will be a bit brighter for you than the last few days. I know it will cheer you up when you know that I haven't got to go further away from you. But cheer up my love, you will soon be here now, won't you, then I'm sure you will feel much better both in health and spirits. I've got several things to tell you but I will leave them until we meet. Please give my love to all at home and my kindest regards to Bertha and Mrs Beale and a nice big kiss for Marjorie and a thousand for yourself. I must close now my darling so with the very best and fondest love and kisses from
Your ever loving Sweetheart

Harold

Xxxxxxxxx
Xxxxxxxxx
Xxxxxxxxx
Xxxxxxxxx

Harold's Army Days

Above: Harold is middle row, on the right.

Left: Harold inset into a brooch. Right: Harold's Cameronian cap badge

Left: Harold and Elsie on their wedding day on November 23rd 1918 in Witham, Braintree, Essex

Right: Harold and Elsie

Harold carried this photograph
of Elsie with him through the
First World War

Chapter 4

Married Life, Work, House Hunting and the Robin Hood, Gallowtree Gate in Leicester

After the war, in the early 1920's Harold and Elsie moved back to Leicester and lived with Harold's aunt and uncle at 54 Pool Road, Leicester. Elsie found this difficult and eventually the couple bought a bungalow at Scraptoft. The Bannerman Road houses mentioned in Harold's letter dated April 22nd 1921 were in Scraptoft, so it is possible that they moved there sometime between 1921 and 1929 where there is a 7 year gap in the letters. The family home from at least 1929 when the children were young, was 8 St Pauls Road, Leicester. Harold worked at the Co-op bakery as a clerk and later as Assistant Manager according to his son Tony. Mr. Cherry seems to have been his boss. Many of Harold's meals were taken at 'The Café' when he was parted from Elsie, and it seems reasonable that this may have been the Co-op café where the staff seemed to know him really well. Elsie stayed at home and bred rabbits and poultry.
Family holidays were taken at Skegness, and Elkstone in Derbyshire, often by Elsie and the children while Harold worked.
It is thought that Elsie may have had rheumatic fever when her children were young and Tony remembers someone called Nancy who came in to look after the children while Elsie was away.

Established 1860 and enrolled under the Industrial Societies Act.
ALL LETTERS TO BE ADDRESSED TO THE SOCIETY AND NOT TO INDIVIDUALS.
Leicester Cooperative Society Limited.
Central Offices. 4, Union Street,
IN REPLY REFER TO
REFERENCE TO YOUR LETTER
Leicester, April 15th 1921.
TEL. 241.
6.45 pm

April 15th 1921
6.45 pm

Darling,
I hope you arrived quite safe. I am writing this just as your train should be arriving in London. I am very anxious to hear that you are all right, I am glad to hear that the Railway strike is put off.
It will be awfully lonely without you, but cheerio dearie, I shall soon be with you.
Heaps of love and every best wish

Yours for ever

Harold
XXXXXXXXXXXXXXXX

This looks like war times doesn't it? Am sending coffee, pills etc posting tomorrow (Saturday).

(No date)

Dearie,

Received your postcard this morning, very glad to hear you got across London alright. Shall be very pleased when I get a nice long letter from you tomorrow morning.

Am sending you some coffee and your pills, let me know if there is anything else you want sending. Will write you a long letter tomorrow, am in a hurry to catch the 11 o/c post now

Best love and wishes

Yours ever

Harold

54 Pool Road
Leicester
18/4/1921

My darling Sweetheart

Just a line or two to thank you for your long loving letter, which I received this morning. I am very sorry to hear you're not feeling very well, I do hope by this time you are much better. Glad to tell you I feel much better than I did when I wrote to you yesterday. I had a good basin of Bovril and sweated it out of me.

Dearie, I sent your bicycle off today by the Great Central, so you should receive by say Wednesday. You will have to fetch it from the station, as they track it at station to station. Note no free delivery, but if you enquire at the booking office about Wednesday night you should get it alright, but dearie, when you sign for it, just have a look and see that it is all right and that no parts are missing because if you don't and anything is wrong, I cannot claim compensation if you have signed for it "In good condition". I took the bell off it and will send it along - perhaps tomorrow. (By the way, if the cycle is damaged or anything is missing don't forget to sign for it "Damaged" in plain writing just above your signature).

Sorry to hear the weather is so wretched, hope it will soon pick up. I know you will get out as much as you can, because that is what you need to make you better. I am hoping to see ever such a nice strong little wife when I come down for a week on Saturday.

It must have been a pretty good row that Arthur had with Edgar Gray to stop him from going there, but perhaps he is like old Bill, he knows of a better hole and is going to it.

I hope you will let me know what you will be wanting in the way of food stuffs so that I can pack you a parcel and send it. I expect your coffee will soon be running low, tell me when to send and you shall have it all there. I keep on wondering if you are getting any Hovis Bread because I know you won't feel very well if you have to keep eating that nasty old white stuff.

Everything here is just about the same. Uncle is out today with the Assistant Superintendant and Aunt is out collecting again now (7o/c). Cassie and George Orme have been here for tea today but had gone when I got home at 6.30.

Hettie and Hilda came for supper last night, and I had to roust them up for not coming to make me a Yorkshire Pudding. Hettie said she was waiting for me to send her a postcard.
You are a dear little darling aren't you and I do miss you so much, but I know it is for your benefit, so I keep on smiling, knowing that it won't be long before I am with you.
When I have finished your letter, I am going down to Uncle Frank's to arrange with him about next Monday's social and perhaps to give him a game of chess if he isn't too busy. I shall have to hurry up and finish as the post goes in a few minutes. Love from all at home.
Very best wishes from Hettie and Hilda, and with heaps of love and wishes from your ever loving sweetheart

Harold
XXXXXXXXXXXX
XXXXXXXXXXXX
My love and wishes to Mr and Mrs Horsies and all the Goslings, big uns and little uns

Harold

54 Pool Road
Leicester
20/4/1921
Thursday 8 o/c Pm

My own darling sweetheart
I am writing this because I have got a lot to tell you but because I feel I must write to you for I know that if you feel as lonely as I do just now, to receive a letter will be joyful, as welcome as flowers in May. Aunt, Uncle and Cecil have gone to the Guild Social and wanted me to go, but I felt just as if I either wanted to go to the Palace with you or be left severely alone and, as I didn't wish to be bored stiff, I diplomatically refused their kind invitation. Chapel entertainments

for me tonight would be like a red rag to a bull; so I set off by starting to read 'The old man in the Corner' by Baroness Orczy (lent by Geo Orme) until I got fed up, then I took Cecil's old bike (the one in our bedroom) (I think this should read "my bedroom") and started pulling that to bits until I mistook my hand for a screw and started unscrewing it, then I chucked that up. Then I thought I would unburden my weary soul by saying sweet nothings to the garden, couldn't get much peace there because the old chap next door (garden) would persist in keeping up a blumming conversation, so how could a bloke communicate with the spirits then (3) *, and as I didn't feel equal to the task of making myself into a portable gramophone, I slunk off back to my lair and now the only thing to do to prevent bloodshed in this highly respectable suburb is to sit down and unload all my imaginary troubles on you, so now you know why I am writing this. Now I'll start writing sensible. (Even my blinking pencil has got the pip, it won't go where I want it to), Cuss it.*

Dear old thing, I hope that by the time you have read my letter up to here, you haven't ordered an aeroplane (I can't spell tonight) and started flying back home in hopes of seeing me before they put me in the padded room.

Dearest, don't be alarmed, I am quite alright, everything is going on just about as usual, very slow, very quiet, the house seems empty without you to liven it up.

Darling, I do hope by now that your digestion and nerves are much better. You won't get much stronger while you are feeling ill and nervy, and I hope, my love, that you will forgive me for giving you that certain lecture in my last letter. You see I can't stop nagging at you even when you go away.

You should have received my parcel and short letter by this time, so I hope you will eat it all and then dream of me.

No word from the Thurmaston house merchant yet and none from Mr Gilbert (Blast 'em).

I wonder if you have been up to see Mr Bult and Harvey (4) yet, give them my kindest regards when you see them. By the way, thinking of Witham and whiskey, the Robin Hood in Gallowtree Gate, until lately kept by Bobby Monk, was sold today by auction to Mesures Bass and Co the brewers for 21,200. Wish I had owned the Robin Hood.

My darling, here I am alone, what a lovely opportunity to sit you on my knee and tell you how much I love you, but there you are, I suppose the same lovely chance will come again when you come back and we must wait patiently until then. But how galling to be parted from each other.
But there, I ought to be writing some cheerful stuff to buck you up, such as telling you of a man that lived 99 years without his wife, and that sort of stuff.
Never mind, my dear old cherub, keep smiling and when I see you a week on Saturday I shall expect to see a great big bonney [stet bonny], strapping wife something like a Scotch fishwife.
Only 8 more days and then comes the day. I know it is 8 because I've just counted them on my fingers.
Give my love to all the folks I know at Oak Villa and all the Goslings big and little and tell them I'm expecting Witham town to celebrate my coming by fetching the Fire Brigade out to meet me, but I hope they won't expect me to wait until they can pinch a horse to pull the fire engine like they did when they had a fire once. I shall have to close now, got strict orders to have the supper ready by 9.30 (its now 9.20) so will close with heaps and heaps of love and kisses and every best wish from your adoring husband
Harold

XXXXXXXXXXXXXXXX
XXXXXXXXXXXXXXXX
XXXXXXXXXXXXXXXX

(Tell Mrs H. not to think this is a newspaper, it's only a short note)
Goodnight my darling, bless you.

54 Pool Road
Leicester
22/4/21

Darling
Just a line or two to thank you very much for the loving welcome letter received this morning.
Very pleased to hear that you are feeling better now and to tell you that I have got over the fit of the blues that I had when I wrote to you last night.
Although you do not say as much, I am greatly of the opinion that you are not as comfortable down there as you might be. Let me know if this is so. Now, about the question of your coming home. That rests with you entirely. If you feel that you will be better by staying down there another week alone and then the week with me, all well and good, by all means stay, but if on the other hand you are not comfortable and you feel that you would sooner be at home, well pack up and come as soon as you like. Just weigh this matter up in your mind and let me know what you think, but please remember you mustn't be persuaded into coming home by the fact that I am lonely. I shall be far happier alone knowing that your stay there is doing you good than I shall be by having you at home and your breaking down. I only want you to do the best for yourself, I don't mind where you go or what it costs, so long as you get better and stronger. If you can suggest anywhere at the seaside or a quiet little place right away in the country, by all means go there, but whatever you do, I must have you comfortable and happy. Just weigh this up in your mind very seriously and let me know what you think.
Ted Croyden has promised to send you on a few things as soon as I let him know what you want, so just hurry along with your requirements and he will post them on straight from there. Went over to see him this afternoon and had a look at the new houses. Haven't heard any more about them yet.
Heard nothing from Mr Cherry or Mr Gilbert about the Bannerman Rd or Mountcastle Rd houses.
Shall have to close now as it is nearly 7 o/c and I want to catch the post.

Best of love and wishes and all that's good
From your ever loving husband
Harold
XXXXXXXX
XXXXXXXX Goodnight my love

54 Pool Road
Leicester
24/4/1921

My own dearest sweetheart
Just a short letter to thank you very much for your loving letter, which I received yesterday dinnertime. You will no doubt wonder why I didn't reply before, but I cannot write a nice letter to you when the house is so full and last night at the office, everybody was buzzing around and I generally like to be alone if I can when I am writing to you. Darling, I am very pleased to hear you are feeling much better now. I hope you keep it up and it is useless to tell you how much I am looking forward to next Saturday. Really it seems ages since I parted with you a week last Friday afternoon but cheerio, my love, it won't be for very much longer.
Dearie, you haven't said yet if it will be convenient to Mr and Mrs Horsnell for me to come to you for a week and you might send me on a Witham time table together with a list of the trains cancelled. You can easily get this on enquiring at the station. Very pleased to hear you are getting out on your bike a good deal now, it will do you good if the weather is nice. Be sure and let me have that list of groceries that you will want, if you haven't already sent it, because Ted wants to have it and get it sent off to you.
On Friday afternoon, on my way to Thurmaston I went round by Birstall and Wanlip, a very nice little bicycle run, which I shall have to take you the first opportunity we get, and I came across a very nice little poultry farm near to Syston, I know you would like to see it.
We have had Hetty, Hilda, Hubert and Willie Whitehead for tea today, quite a nice little crush. All of them and practically all of Harvey Lane Guild wish to be very kindly remembered to you. Aunt came home with quite a string of names of folks that had been enquiring after your health. Last week I have seen Fred Hand and Gertie and each

time they haven't offered to speak and Gertie looks at me as savage as if she could eat me. I don't know why. Arthur doesn't seem to be having very good luck with his chickens does he? Everybody here, except Uncle and I, have gone to Chapel. My word it is quiet and lonely, the place seems to empty and deserted, won't it be lovely to have you back again and every time I go to bed at night, I feel more lonely still when I haven't got you to love and talk to, but never mind, it will only be for 5 more days and then....
When I see you on Saturday, I shall expect to see you ever so much better and so much happier and free from all those horrible aches and pains that used to spoil practically every day of your life.
But my love, these little troubles will be greatly lessened when we get a house of our own and when you will be able to do just as you like without being afraid of hurting people's feelings.
So cheerio my little darling, and keep wishing for Saturday to come around.
Love to all at Witham
Best wishes to you from all at Leicester and heaps and heaps of love and kisses and best wishes from your ever loving hubby

Harold
XXXXXXXXXXXXXXX
XXXXXXXXXXXXX

No Address
May 5/1921

Dearest
Just a line to wish you very many happy returns of the day, with every good wish for your health and happiness, with fondest love from
Yours ever

Harold
XXXXXXXX
XXXXXXXX

Chapter 5
1929 – A Family, the Café, the Roll Top Desk, First 'Talkie' Movie, and the Trip.

By the time their daughter Pamela was born on July 11th 1926, Harold and Elsie had a drapery shop and were living at 48 Braunstone Gate, Leicester, although Harold continued working at the Co-op as a Baker's clerk. When Harold contracted scarlet fever in April 1928 and became seriously ill he was expected to die. Their second child was due to be born during this time and if a boy, was to be called Peter. Because of Harold's expected imminent death, the child, born on April 26th 1928, was named 'Harold' after his father. Harold survived and baby Harold was always known as Peter, and later in life as 'Pete'. Anthony (Tony) arrived on April 24th 1930. Elsie may well have been suffering from morning sickness, possibly reflected in Harold's references to her health. She appears to have gone away with the children to recuperate. Peter and Tony were both born at 8 St Pauls Road, the family home in Leicester.

Harold, Elsie, Pamela and Peter, Tony was an inside passenger on this photograph.

H. Hartell
8 St Pauls Road
Leicester
Sept 2/1929
10.5 am

Darling
Glad to tell you I arrived home quite safely just before 11o/c. Had a cup' tea [stet cup of tea] and a piece of bread and butter in bed. The weather looks like being good again today. I hope you and the kiddies have a good time. I don't care very much for being a bachelor, but shall not mind if only it makes you better. I hope the kiddies didn't give you too much trouble after I left, perhaps you will be answering a lot of questions about Daddy today. I am going to have my breakfast when I have written this. Just had time for a cup tea this morning, didn't get up until after 8 o/c and had to be here at 9 o/c sharp as Bill is away today.
I am counting the days until I see you again, bless you. Kiss the kiddies for me and tell them I will soon be coming back to you all. Saw Mrs S this morning and she wanted to know if you were alright. I will write again tonight or tomorrow morning and let you know how I am getting on.
Heaps of love and kisses darling, and keep smiling

Yours ever
Harold

8 St Pauls Road
Leicester
Sept 2 1929

Darling Sweetheart
Bless you for your most welcome letter which arrived before I got home tonight. I have had my meals at the Café, so have nothing else to do but go to bed when I have been to post this letter. The weather has been grand here today, I hope it has been as good

there; the kiddies would have a good time, just the weather for their bathing costumes and paddling. I got the roll top desk and revolving chair home this afternoon. I didn't know where it will go best, it's a tight fit as it is now, perhaps Aggie will suggest moving the things round when she is here on Friday morning. I intended to sow that grass seed tonight but I can't find it anywhere. Perhaps I'll be more successful tomorrow. I wish to heaven it was a week next Friday, I'm fed up with wandering about, the house is so dreadfully quiet. I've just been and chopped some wood to relieve my feelings. When I see you next week I shall expect to see you all as brown as berries and you strong and well enough to carry me back home. Don't forget that oysters are now in season, and they are not at all fattening. I wonder if you mentioned to Mrs Parkins about my coming next week. It didn't dawn on me that I hadn't told her that I was staying next week. Don't forget to let me know when you want some more money, and please don't deny yourself anything that you would like, because I will send you more if you will only send the word.

Cheer up sweetheart and have a good time, so that you are heaps better when I see you. Only 11 days now.

Kiss the children for me and tell Pamela that I am working to get some money to come and see her soon. I will write to you tomorrow and let you know any news. It is 9 o/c now and when I have walked down to the GPO (General Post Office) I shall go to bed and think of you my angel and hope the time will not be long before I see you. Keep well my precious, you know that I love you more than all the world and life is hardly worthwhile without you, but I am trying to only think of when I shall see you again.

All my love and kisses sweetheart

Yours for ever

Harold

Above: Harold's roll top desk which may have come from the Co-op, passed down to his grandson in Nottingham

8 St Pauls Road
Leicester
3/9/1929

My Darling Sweetheart
I hope you are keeping well. I didn't have a letter today, perhaps it will be here tomorrow morning. I have had it into my head today that you were not as well. If that is so, I wish you would see a doctor right away. I had a real slap-up lunch today, in fact it was a dinner. One of the regular diners was celebrating his success in accountancy exams. Here is the menu:

Orange slices
Lobster salad
Grouse, K beans, poto fritters
Pineapple creams
Biscuits, cheese
Coffee
Champagne (only a sip)
A real good feed, served gloriously.

The weather has been bad here today, raining in heavy showers for the most part, a rather heavy thunder storm about 2 o/c. I hope it has been better at your end. I hope the kiddies are having a good time. I should love to see them. Chin up my sweetheart, it is not much more that a week now before I see you. I hope time will pass quickly. Is there anything you are wanting? Just let me know if you have thought of anything you wish you had bought.
I have bought two shirts, a hat, a pair of golf hose today at Morgan Squires, quite nice ones, but my pocket is much lighter now.
Had a letter from Mr Cherry today. He is having a good time with splendid weather. I think I will post this letter first thing in the morning. Perhaps I shall have had some news from you by then and if there is anything you are wanting I can send word straight back. I have an idea you will get it nearly as quick as if I posted it tonight.
I am looking to hear that you are well, in fact a lot better than when I left you.
I don't think I have any more news, only to tell you that I am still counting the days until I see you. Only ten more now.
Cheer up my darling, I will tell you how much I love you when I see you. Kiss the children for me, I hope they are good for you, and that Pam is not worrying too much for Daddy. I expect the wine will be due by this time next week. I shall bring a bottle of port with me if it has. It might help to buck you up.

8.45 am Wed Morning.
I have got your welcome letter this morning. Very glad to hear that you are feeling better. You all look well on the photograph. I am hoping that this will really put you on your feet again. It certainly looks as if it is Skegness air that you need. We shall have to see

about you living there 6 months each year and me coming over at weekends, but oh, the weeks. Aggie has evidently been in and cleaned up yesterday. She couldn't have liked the look of my bed when I had made it because she did it again. I shall take your snapshot into Mrs Stonestreet's for the children. I know they are wanting to know how you all are. I don't think there is anything else I can tell you. It is now 9.10 and I shall have to pack up and go. I didn't get up until 8.30 this morning, so there is a scurry round. I am hoping you get this by teatime today. I shall be thinking of you.
Chin up sweetheart, until I see you, which won't be long.
All my love and kisses, yours forever

Harold

8 St Pauls Road
Leicester
4/9/1929
8.45pm

Darling Sweetheart
I have had two letters from you today, one this morning and the other was here when I got home tonight. I am ever so glad to know you are feeling stronger and not so depressed. That will help you to keep going until I see you. Aggie had just been in for the shirts, she had your letter this afternoon, she is going to bring them back in the morning so that I can change them tomorrow night. I have got my suit and I think it looks quite nice. I am putting most of the things in the big case tonight. I thought of putting both our luggage in the one suitcase to save carrying, but I haven't seen Mr Stonestreet yet.
They are looking after me all right at the Café, I had steamed lemon sole and parsley sauce, pots and beans and stewed plums for dinner today, and a fruit mixture for tea. They are worse than you for seeing that I don't have anything that I shouldn't, they cook the vegetables separately without salt and they give me what they think is good for me and not what I came to ask for. I have made a fire and am going to have a bath, as no doubt I shall be chasing round tomorrow night to make sure I haven't forgotten anything. I have

promised to go to the Granby tomorrow night with Miss G. and Sally, to see 'Follies of 1929' so I shall have to behave myself. They even had the cheek to tell me that they ate up all the griller ham and tomatoes so that I shouldn't have any and they made me have the fruit instead. I am ever so glad the kiddies are enjoying themselves, but rather surprised they have been paddling. I thought they would have been afraid of the water. Have a good time my Darling as you have got the winter in front of you and you will want all your energy for the hard work you will have to do with the children. I haven't very much news tonight. I will leave this letter open and let you know anything that crops up tomorrow morning and post it at the GPO about 10 o/c.
Goodnight my sweetheart sleep well and I hope the weather keeps good so that you can spend every minute out of doors.
All my love and wishes
Yours for ever
Harold

8.45 am Thursday
I have just got your letter that you wrote at 6 o/c last night. Sorry to hear that you were not well, are you sure you feel all right again? Mr and Mrs Stonestreet came in last night and fixed up the final details about tomorrow. I shall write you again tonight and will send you a P.C. (postcard).

8 St Pauls Road
Leicester
5/9/1929
11.0 pm

Darling Sweetheart
I got your letter this morning, written on Tuesday night. I am sorry to hear you have not been well. I hope you are feeling better now and that you don't have it again.
Today has been another glorious day, I hope you have enjoyed it. I am glad you went when you did, my darling, so that you could have the benefit of this beautiful weather, not that I wouldn't sooner have

you here with me, but you would have felt so ill and the children would have bothered you to death, but you know that I don't want to be without you, don't you my love? But I hope to make you well and strong again. I saw your Papa today in Union St for the first time in many months and Jim is working as a labourer on the same job. I went to the Granby with Miss G and Sally tonight to see 'Follies of 1929' a Movietone talking, singing film, it was ever so good, and I quite enjoyed my first "talkie", although I must admit that when the first words came through it seemed rather supernatural until I got used to it. I wished the fellow and girl in front of me hadn't insisted on spooning, it put me off my stroke a bit, with me being a lonely, miserable, grumpy bachelor. I have been and seen Mr Stonestreet tonight and arranged the final details for tomorrow. We leave Leicester at 11.38, get to St Pancras at 1.25, get across to Waterloo and leave there (if we catch the train) at 1.50 arriving at Southsea about 3.30pm. I thought I would give you the times as I know you will be thinking of me. I will send you a line as soon as we get to Southsea to let you know I arrived safely. The address we are staying at is:

Mrs Kingston
9 Northcote Road
Fawcett Road
Southsea.

The wine has come and when I come to you next Friday I shall bring either 1 bottle or 2 bottles with me so that you can have some with some phosferine in it. Only 7 more days my sweetheart and then we shall be together again, and I hope it will not be necessary to part again. You have no idea how I am longing to see you. I hope the kiddies are enjoying themselves, I should love to see them. I am afraid I haven't anymore news tonight. So goodnight my sweetheart, sleep well, knowing that you have all my love and wishes

Yours for ever

Harold XXXXXXXXXXXX and some more

Chapter 6
The Schneider Trophy, Isle of Wight, 1929

In these letters Harold has taken a trip to the Isle of Wight to see the The Schneider Trophy event. The Trophy was awarded annually (and later, biannually) to the winner of a race for sea-planes and flying boats from 1913 to 1931. In 1929 the contest was held on September 7th in England, at Calshot. The start and finish of the 186 mile course was located at Cowes on the Isle of Wight with turning points at Sea View, a point about 6 miles South of Hayling Island and Southsea (5). Harold gives a detailed account of his visit to the event. Elsie went to Skegness with the children while he was away.

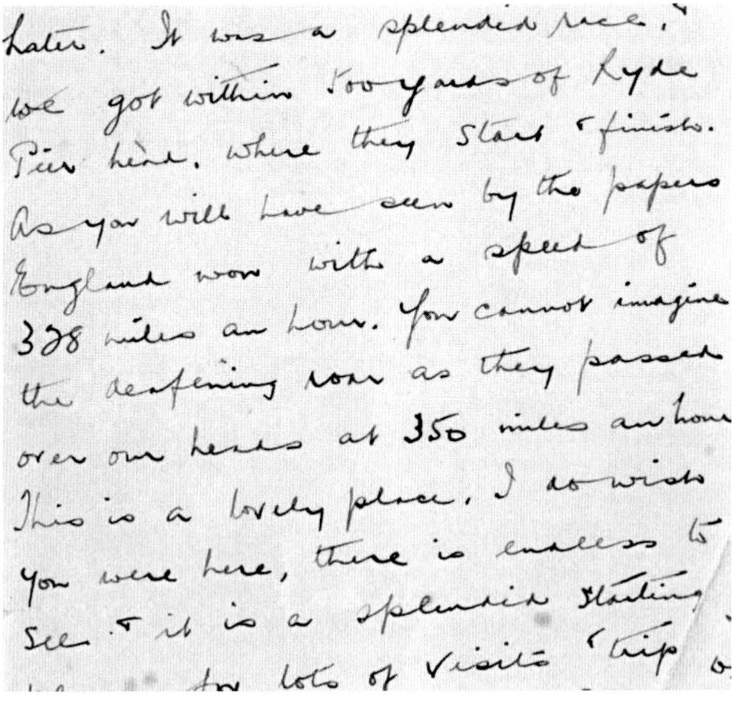
later. It was a splendid race.
We got within 500 yards of Ryde
Pier head, where they start & finish.
As you will have seen by the papers
England won with a speed of
328 miles an hour. You cannot imagine
the deafening roar as they passed
over our heads at 350 miles an hour
This is a lovely place, I do wish
you were here, there is endless to
see & it is a splendid Skating
for lots of visits & trip

9 Northcote Rd
Southsea
7/9/1929
10.30am

Dearest
I hope you have received my letter by now and that you are all right. Southsea is a beautiful place and it is full of people. I have never seen so many young people at a place before. The place seems crowded with young girls. We have just taken tickets for a boat trip out to the course. We start at 11.45 so we should be on the sea for a good time today, as the race is expected to last until about 4.30. The Daily Mail is broadcasting music as we sit here on the pier waiting for the boat to come in. We had a very nice sea trip round the Ports and Italian Warships last night. We were out about 1 ½ hours and it was very nice. There are some nice liners and yachts out here anchored to see the race.

Later. *It was a splendid race, and we got within 500 yards of Ryde Pier Head where they start and finish. As you will have seen by the papers England won with a speed of 328 miles an hour. You cannot imagine the deafening roar as they passed over our heads at 350 miles an hour.*
This is a lovely place. I do wish you were here, there is endless to see, and it is a splendid starting place for lots of visits and trips.
I hope you have had a good day and that the children are enjoying themselves. As we shall be leaving here early on Tuesday morning, I wouldn't address any letters to here after you get this (which I hope will be first post on Monday). It is just a week come tomorrow since I left you and it seems at least a month. I hope the next 6 days doesn't seem as long. Only another 6 days and then we shall be together again. I am not likely to forget this fortnight for a while. If this writing looks wiggled, don't think I am canned, I am writing this sitting in a deck chair on the pier and it isn't the best place for writing.
Kiss the children for me and tell them I shall soon be with them now. Heaps of love and kisses my darling until I see you.

Goodnight my love, sleep well and I hope you are feeling ever so much better.
Yours for ever

Harold

9 Northcote Rd
Southsea
9/9/1929

My Dear Sweetheart
I hope you have received my letter by now. You wouldn't get one from Saturday morning until this afternoon, and it's too long to wait, isn't it. I haven't had one from you since I left Leicester, last Friday, but I hope there will be one waiting for me when arrive home tomorrow (Tuesday) night. I am writing this on Cowes Pier (I.O.W.) while waiting for the boat to take us back to the mainland. It is a very nice place but very hilly.
We have arrived back again (at 7 o/c) and we are now on the pier. The Hampshires' Band is playing. There is not much chance of writing a long letter here, there are people all around walking and talking. Mr Stonestreet has got very brown with the sun. I have only just caught it a bit on the forehead. We are catching the 9.58 train tomorrow (Tuesday) morning for Waterloo, getting there at 11.39 and we shall be leaving St Pancras somewhere about 8 o/c at night. I will write you a card at London which I hope you will get on Wednesday morning. By the time you get this, it will only be another 3 days before I see you. I wish it was not so long, I am getting impatient for next Friday night to come. I am longing to see you my darling and I know you are longing to see me. I will make up for lost time when I see you, my angel. I feel a bit of a pig for not writing yesterday but really there is no chance to be alone and quiet to write a nice loving letter and I don't want to write a postcard with just ordinary greetings on it. I am hoping there will be a letter from you for me when we get home tonight as I feel as if I haven't heard from you for ever so long.

Goodnight my sweetheart, sleep well, and when I see you on Friday night I hope to find you ever so much better than when I left you and the kiddies all brown and happy. Kiss them for me and tell Pam that her Daddy will soon be with her again. By the way, I don't know if I told you the time I get in on Friday night. I shall leave here at 5.11 and get to Skegness at 7.58 pm. That is if Mc will let me off on the Friday evening, if not I shall have to come by the Saturday morning bus, but I am hoping that won't be necessary.
All my love and kisses, my angel.
Yours for ever

Harold

Friday morn
(No date)

Darling
I have just got your letter written last night. Glad to know you are keeping better and that the children are enjoying themselves. This time next week, my love, I shall be counting the hours until I see you, I shall arrive in Skegness by the 7.58 train.
Cheerio my darling, keep smiling until I see you
Heaps of love and kisses
Yours

Harold

8 St Pauls Road
Leicester
10/9/1929
8.45pm

My Darling Sweetheart
Thank you ever so much for your lovely letter which was at home when I arrived at 7 o/c this evening. Mrs Stonestreet got me to send

a postcard to you almost as soon as we got in and Marjorie posted it for me. I hope you get this one at the same time.

Only 3 more nights, my angel, before we are together. I am longing to see you and tell you how much I have missed you. I certainly shall not think of taking a travelers' job on after this little lot. I am ever so glad to hear that you're feeling better again. Keep well my sweetheart, and if there is anything you want, don't hesitate to get it, and if you want any money before Friday night just drop me a line and I will send it straight on. I am hoping to make a nice lot of money this winter, so that you won't have to have such a rough time of it in the future as you have done in the past. Aggie has brought me a clean shirt and as I have only used one of my 2 new ones, I shall be quite all right for them. I will bring the serviettes and the Sanatogen with me together with a bottle of port. Darling, why not get a tin of Sanatogen tomorrow and use it straight away, instead of waiting until Friday night. I hope you have been able to get out by yourself at nights so that you could have a change. Kiss the kiddies for me and tell Pam that Daddy is hurrying to you all as fast as he can. When you get this it will be only two more nights before I am with you and then I shall be able to tell you how much I love you. Bless you my precious angel.

It is just after 9 o/c now and I am just going to the GPO to post this letter and then I shall go to bed and think of my darling sweetheart, who is the dearest little soul in all the world.

Goodnight my angel, sleep well and count the hours until Friday night 7.58 pm

All my love and kisses
Yours for ever

Harold

XXXXXXXXXXXX

Chapter 7

Back at Work, the Café, Negotiating Holidays, Tony arrives and Elsie's Surgery.

In the letter dated May 1st 1930 it appears that Elsie was in hospital after giving birth to Tony, her third child. On October 28th the same year she was again in hospital having had surgery. Harold's letters indicate that he was looking after the children with the help of friends and relatives. Elsie remained in hospital for almost two weeks.

Harold with one of the children

8 St Pauls Road
Leicester
11/9/1929
4.0pm

My Darling Sweetheart
Here we are, back at work again. It isn't so bad being at work, the time passes quicker and Friday night will come all the sooner. By the time you get this there will only be one more night before we are together. Won't that be splendid? I have never looked forward to anything as I am looking forward to seeing you. It seems ages since I left you but I will make up for it when I do see you. Aggie came in this morning before I went to work. She has washed my old coloured shirt, and has taken my silk vest to put a patch on it. You wouldn't believe the rude things she said when I suggested cutting the torn part off. She said she had expected to hear from you but she hadn't. I hope you are feeling well my darling and that the change is doing you good. I expect the kiddies are getting nice and brown by now. I shall love to see them. I hope they are not too tiresome for you. Do you think you will be able to leave them in bed while we go for a stroll last thing at night next week, because you never get a chance of going out without them if not. If there is anything else you wish me to bring with me just let me know and I'll bring it along all right. Mr Cherry had a good holiday and looks and feels much better for it. Miss Griffin is going to Newquay, where Mr Cherry went, on Saturday morning. I am still having my meals at the Café. I had shredded wheat and hot milk for breakfast and chicken and vegetables and plums and custard for dinner. I don't know what they will give me for tea yet, but they are looking after me very well, apart from the cheek I have to put up with. I was very glad to sleep in our own little bed last night. It was better than being in a strange place and you couldn't expect Mr Stonestreet to sympathize with a fellow that's feeling lonely. By the way I think they were in bed before 10 o /c last night - I don't think I have any more news for you this time, my love. I will write again tomorrow and then I hope to forget how to write letters to you sweetheart.

Fondest love and kisses my darling, and when you get this, there will only be one more day before we are together, won't that be grand?
All my love

Yours for ever

Harold

H. Hartell
8 St Pauls Road
Leicester
12/9/1929

Darling sweetheart
I got your letter written yesterday afternoon, this morning, for which, heaps of kisses. I think I have done everything you said in your letter and last night I got most of my things put in the case. Tonight I shall complete it, and then I shall be ready to start on my journey to you. By the time you get this, my darling, it will only be a few hours before I am with you, won't that be splendid. I have got all the things you asked for in your letter, and I am trying not to forget anything I ought to bring.
It is all O.K. about my coming tomorrow by the 5.11, I asked Mr Cherry first before I mentioned it to Mc, in case he refused, in which case I should have had to tell him that I had already got the necessary permission, artful dodger. I hope you sleep well tonight, my sweetheart. I don't think I shall, I shall be thinking of all the things I am going to tell you when I see you, I don't mean news. By the way, I didn't get your second letter at Southsea. It must have got there after we left, but we left our addresses with Miss Kingston,

so she will post it on to me. Perhaps it will be there when I get home tonight. I haven't been home in the day time since you have been away. I hope you have had another good day. The weather has been beautifully hot again here, and I hope the children are making the most of their chances. Kiss the kiddies for me and tell Pamela that Daddy will be with her before she goes to bed again. I am ever so glad to hear you are feeling better. I hope you will continue so.

I haven't much news, and what there is will do when I see you. Sleep well my sweet heart and I will very soon be with you now. Only 28 hours now darling.
All my love and kisses
Yours for ever

Harold

8 St Pauls Road
Leicester
May 1/1930

Darling Sweetheart
Just a line or two hoping they will cheer you up and help you along until I see you again on Saturday. I am ever so glad to see you are getting on so well and hope you will continue to make good progress when you get home again. Cheer up my love, it will soon be Wednesday, and then we shall be together again, and I shall have a chance to tell you how much I love you. I haven't been able to say a nice word to you with all those other people around, but I hope to make up all the lost time before long. I have just got home (8.30)

and when I have written or posted this to the dearest little sweetheart in all the world, I shall have a bath and go to bed, for there is nothing else to do. You have no idea how lonely I feel when you are not here, it seems just as if I were in a strange house in a strange town. How much easier it would be to tell you what I should like to say to you, than it is to write it. It is an effort to make this letter of reasonable length, but I could tell you enough to fill a book.
I met Hilda on my way home and she asked very kindly after you and said they had received your postcard. I shall call on Aggie tomorrow and tell her to bring the flannels and binders you asked for. You might just impress upon her the privilege she has been granted when she visits you tomorrow. I don't know of anyone else that I would stand down for, and she will have to be on her best behaviour tomorrow or I won't let her come at all. I hope she will be able to tell you that Billy has got on well at his new job, it will be a load off her mind to know that he has a chance of a fairly certain, regular job. As I haven't anything further I can tell you, I must end this little note, but not before I repeat my everlasting love for the sweetest dearest wife that ever lived. Roll on next Wednesday, and then I shall be the happiest man in the world.
Love and kisses for Anthony, and all my love and wishes for you, my sweetheart.

Harold

8 St Pauls Road
Leicester
Oct 28 /1930

Darling Sweetheart
Just a line to cheer you up. I have been wondering all day how you have been getting on. It is 5.45 now. Tony has just gone to bed; he has been a good boy today. Mrs Stoneshill has been in and supervised Betty getting him undressed. Aggie came in this afternoon to see if she could do anything for us. I am hoping that when I come to see you tomorrow afternoon, your ordeal will have

been all over. I have already counted the days between now and when you come home again, which I hope will be a week on Saturday.
Pam and Peter have been good children today, they are taking it very well indeed so far. I don't think they will be very much trouble if they go on as they are at present. They are playing on the floor just now with dead matches. I hope you are not feeling too bad and getting a good read in bed. I haven't been out this afternoon, just messing about, it seems a terribly long day today. I am missing you terribly, but I know that it will be for your good, so we must put up with being parted for a while. I don't think I have any more to tell you just now, everything is going on about the same here.
All my love and best wishes my darling, until I see you tomorrow. Try to get as much sleep as you can. You will want all your strength to get well again. Heaps of love and kisses sweetheart
From yours for ever

Harold

H. Hartell
8 St Pauls Road
Leicester
Nov 2 /1930
2.15pm

My Darling Sweetheart
I hope you are still making good progress. I am hoping you will be at home this time next week, for the house seems like nothing on earth since you have been away. I hope you have had a nice dinner, we have had the remains of the chicken and an apple pie. The children have just gone to call for Joan, they are going on the park and Betty is going across with Tony when she has washed up.
Aunt came in this morning. She still has a bad cold. Bill Upton and Ralph came in as well, to say that Aggie has a bad cold and to ask the name of your ward. Nothing else was mentioned. I hope it won't be long before next Wednesday, I shall miss my nightly visit.

Keep smiling darling, in about a week's time you should be home again and there is such a lot I want to tell you. The children are quite alright, they seem to be eating better again just now. Tony's botty has nearly healed, he is a good boy until nearly feed time and then he lets it go. I am sending you a few apples and oranges, they are Coxes Orange Pippin from Simpkins. We have fixed you a bed in the middle room, but when you get home, perhaps you will suggest moving the things around a bit, as we don't know just how to put them all for the best. If there is anything else you are wanting, just drop me a line, and I will send it right along.
Keep smiling my angel, you know how much I love you and I am longing to have you back home and I hope you will very soon be strong again.
All my love and kisses, my sweetheart, until I see you on Wednesday.
Yours ever

Harold

H. Hartell
8 St Pauls Road
Leicester
Nov 3 /1930

Darling Sweetheart
Thank you ever so much for your lovely letter, I got it when I got home to dinner. Poor old angel, I quite realise what a rotten day you had yesterday, words cannot describe my feelings all day yesterday. It was the most miserable Sunday I have ever spent. Never mind love, I hope you will spend the next one at home, and then it won't be so lonely. I am delighted to learn you are feeling better, keep that up and we shall soon be happy. I read the letters to Pam and Peter and their little faces beamed, bless them. I'm hoping that by now (6 o/c) that you will have had the stitches out and I only hope they did not hurt so much as I have imagined they would. It is a shame I cannot kiss you better, but that is only a pleasure deferred.

I am sending you two cuttings from the Sunday Express, I hope you will like them. Mr and Mrs is very good this week. It seems a long time until Wednesday, I hope the time until then goes quicker than it has done since Saturday. If there is anything else you are wanting darling, just drop me a line, I shall be glad of an excuse to come along, even if it is only as far as the patient's lounge. I am also sending you a book Harry Jay bought for me this afternoon, I hope you will like it. Sir Phlliip Gibbs made him the chief character in it, he is named 'Cherry of Lynchbung'. I haven't read it but by odd lines I have come across, it seems a very good description of him. Keep smiling my angel, it will soon be the end of the week, at least I'm hoping it will.

Fondest love and kisses

Yours Ever

Harold

8 St Pauls Road
Leicester
Nov 4 /1930
6 o/c pm

Darling Sweetheart

Bless you my angel for your lovely letter, which I received this morning. So sorry to hear that you were not feeling so well after they had taken the clips out, I hope you are feeling better by now, my love. Did you get the flowers last night? I hope they sent them straight up to you. You should have had them by about 6 o/c. I have given your message about Miss Freer to Cissy, she was very surprised, as she saw her not many days ago. Mrs Hogg is sending you some grapes with me tomorrow with her best wishes for a speedy recovery. I am anxiously waiting for tomorrow, it is the longest 4 days I can remember. I am longing to see you my sweetheart, I shall be glad more than you can imagine to have you home again. The new stove has been fitted today, so we are all ready to welcome you home. If there is anything you want me to

bring you tomorrow, just drop me a line, my angel, and I will bring it along.
All the neighbours send their love and best wishes to you.
The children are quite all right at the moment, they are sitting on the hearth watching Jack put the missing tile in the range hearth. Tony is just off to bed, I have kissed him for you. I know you would love to see them, so you shall my love, in a few more days.
Keep smiling my darling one. You know I love you more than everything else on earth, and I am just longing to have you to myself. There is not much news tonight, I must hurry or they won't send this up to you tonight. I should like you to know that I dearly love you before you settle down for the night. Tomorrow afternoon will not be long now my precious and you can bet I shall be there on stroke of half past two.
Goodnight my darling one, all my love and wishes until I see you.
Bless you, my angel.
Yours ever

Harold

XXX Kisses from Pam
XXX kisses from Peter
XXX Kisses from Daddy

Goodnight Sweetheart

8 St Pauls Road
Leicester
Nov 6 /1930
2.00 pm

Darling
I hope you are feeling better today and that the stitches will not be too painful.
I am trying to get everything straight and tidy in time for Saturday in case you do come home then, but I am rather afraid we shall have to be patient until Monday. I am sending you a clean towel and some stamps as requested. If there is anything else, just let me know. I

saw the porter yesterday when I left you and he put me right about ordering the Ambulance. Aggie came in last night, and her father is very ill, Gastric Flu.

The children are quite well, and send their love and kisses. All the usual friends send their love and best wishes. I must hop off to work now, we are going to do the bedrooms when I come back.

All my love and kisses until I see you on Saturday

Yours ever

Harold

H. Hartell
8 St Pauls Road
Leicester
Nov 7 /1930

Darling Sweetheart

Sorry to hear you will not be home until Tuesday at the earliest, that means another lonely weekend, but never mind angel, we shall be together once more before very long. The kiddies are quite well, and things are going on pretty well. We didn't get the bedrooms done yesterday, but I hope today. There isn't very much news to tell today. I am trying to get this and the choclolate rolls up to you before you have your tea today. Cheer up sweetheart, with good luck we should be together again in 4 or 5 more days, and then we can make up the time we have been parted. It has seemed a terribly long time, but if you feel much better afterwards, it will have been worth it. It won't be long now until tomorrow, my precious, all my love and kisses darling one, until then

Yours for ever

Harold

8 St Pauls Road
Leicester
9/11 /1930
2.15pm
3.00pm

Darling Sweetheart
It won't be long now my angel before you are home again. It doesn't seem such a long day today as it did last Sunday. Aunt came in this morning and took Peter back with her until this evening, and Pam and I went to Scraptoft this morning to get a bell push from Mr Taylor.
We have got some nice chicken for your dinner tomorrow and a plum pie. Don't forget to ask the nurse what you should have to eat, as we don't want to give you anything that will do you harm. I saw the Hall Porter just after I left you yesterday and fixed up for the ambulance for 10.30am so I shall see you about that time. Dr. Badenoch doesn't sit on Saturday evenings, so I shall get him to fix up a district nurse. I think we shall have everything ready for when you come home, and I don't intend to go back to work until 6 o/c and then only for about half an hour. I have such a lot to tell you, my precious, that I don't think I shall go to bed very early, if at all. Pam is coming with me to bring this letter. She is going to give it to the porter and tell him to be sure to give it to her Mummy. There isn't very much to tell. I am too excited at the thoughts of having you to myself again, I couldn't even kiss you unexpectedly in that ward with all those people looking, but oh boy, won't I kiss you properly when I get you home. Pamela sends you three kisses, here they are.
XXX
I will save mine until tomorrow. All my love and kisses my darling angel until tomorrow.
By the way, the name of the play at the Opera this week is called "Nearly a honeymoon", it won't be necessary for us to go and see it;
Cheerio my love
Yours for ever

Harold

Chapter 8
Elkstone, Derbyshire 1933

To write his letter dated 25th of July 1933 Harold used paper with the following name and address printed on the reverse side.

G.H. Cherry
37 Evington Lane
Leicester

It was written to Elsie when she was staying at a farmhouse in Elkstone in Derbyshire where some holidays were taken and where Elsie and the children were staying in the summer of 1933. The children were able to ride horses on the farm and Tony has happy memories of Elkstone. Mr. and Mrs. Davenport either lived or stayed there and had a shared interest in astrology with Elsie.

8 St Pauls Rd
Leicester
25/7/1933
10.20pm

My Darling
I hope you have had another fine, happy and useful day and that you had a good night's sleep. I went to bed last night (Monday) at 12 o/c and I was still asleep at 9 o/c this morning. It was a few minutes to 10 o/c when I got to the office. You will be interested to know that I went in the car and delivered bread to John Myers at the wooden bungalow he has built on the land he has at Brookside, Station Road, Thurnby. He took me all over his land, but I did not let on that I knew quite a lot about it. I have had lunch and tea with Mr Banks, and I shall have some Corn Flakes before I go to bed (11.30 no I won't). I am writing this drinking tea and listening to the wireless broadcasting dance music and wondering if you are listening too.

The weather has been scorching hot here today. I hope it has been nice at Elkstone, that you and the children are getting really well and strong. Only 4 more days, my angel, and then I shall come along and be with you again. Won't that be jolly. This seems a jolly long week. Fancy it being only yesterday morning since I kissed you goodbye. Never mind, sweetheart mine, I will make up for our loneliness when we get home. Kindly remember me to Mr and Mrs Davenport. I hope you have been able to have some interesting and helpful chats about astrology. It will help to pass the time away for you, and you may learn something from them or their books. I'm afraid I haven't very much news to tell you tonight, Sweetheart, nothing unusual has happened. I haven't been at home so far, so haven't had any visitors. I saw Mrs Ansell this morning, and she was glad to hear that you and the children were comfortable and having good weather.

Have a good time, my darling Sweetheart, there will be enough work when you get back into your stride and get nice and strong so that you can face the winter better than you have been able to do the last year or two

Goodnight my Sweetheart, all my love and kisses and every good wish for you and the children.

Yours ever

Harold

XXXXXXXXXXXX

Chapter 9
Harold's Illness, and Convalescence in Southport near Liverpool, Merseyside, Lancashire.

In 1935 Harold and Elsie built a house at Newtown Linford, Leicestershire. They named their home 'Uranus' through Elsie's interest in astrology. The astrological sign was carved into the gates at the front of the house. The family moved to their new home sometime in 1937 just before Harold became ill.

In February 1938, Harold's letters were written from a convalescent home in Southport. It is known that he had two strokes and his mention of having treatment for arm and shoulder weakness and the use of a sling would support this. An insight is given into the treatment regime he received for his condition as well as the diet provided by the home. Harvey, a family friend, seemed to be a great support to Harold at the time of his illness, and Theosophy became more prominent.

Room 40
Southport Convalescent hospital
Seabanks Rd
Southport
No date
Sat 3.0 pm

My Darling
Here we are again, I hope you are quite alright and feeling not too bad. If I don't settle down in a few days I shall be right home again pretty quick. The place is quite alright, every body is very kind and willing to help but I am not appreciating institution life a bit just now. I went to bed at 8.45 last night having nothing to do, and thinking of you all the time. Sleep was impossible until early morning and we have to be up at 6.0 am. Just imagine me up at that time.
Breakfast is at 8.0, dinner at 12.0, tea at 4.0, supper at 8.0. The weather here has not been too good yet, dull, trying to rain, and quite a strong breeze blowing, not at all comfortable for trying to walk, nothing to do all day long. I had a massage this morning on the arm and I go on Tuesday for a shoulder massage at 9.30 am. The massage is very gentle and just perhaps 10 minutes, so you can see it will take a long time at this rate to make much progress. Still I suppose I must expect it to affect me for the first few days, but I hope this horrible feeling will soon pass off and that I shall begin to feel better otherwise it is a sheer waste of time and emotion. I hope the next letter you receive will be in a more cheerful view. By the way, can you tell me how much silver you gave me? Give my love and kisses to the children, I want to write them each a little letter if I can manage it before I get too tired and depressed. Being on what they call a special diet I had bread and milk for supper last night, porridge for breakfast and tripe for dinner. Nearly everybody is complaining of being unable to sleep, through bronchitis cases who cough and groan nearly all night. Please don't take too much notice of my moaning attitude, it will pass off soon I hope. I never was one for leaving home and forgetting my dear family. It is now nearly 4 o/c and I am going to make my way toward the dining room before the crush start going in.

Sunday 9.30 am. How did you sleep my dear? I had a much better night owing to the poor chap in the next cubicle having been sent away. He has been here about 3 months and they can do him no good. In bed by 9.0 pm and did not hear the gale and the rain that has been on all night. Breakfast a boiled egg at 8.0 am. Just imagine me having breakfast at that unearthly hour. The wind is still blowing half a gale but it is quite sunny now. I don't think I shall [stet go] out this morning while the wind is on. Have got the Sunday Express so shall go and have a quiet read for a while. I don't feel quite so horribly despondent this morning. Hope I shall be able to get used to it very soon. I wish the fortnight was over already, it does not seem to be living to be in such strange surroundings. I miss you more and more each day that goes so slowly along. I want to write a little letter to the children to put in with this letter today. I won't write anymore to this or I won't have anything to say tomorrow. Bless you my love, look after yourself and don't attempt that spring cleaning. Fix your mind on Friday week and let's hope it won't seem too long.
All my love and kisses your adoring hubby

Harold

Room 40
Southport Convalescent hospital
Seabanks Rd
Feb 28th 1938

My Darling
It was grand to get a letter from you this morning, it reminded me of days long ago. Very pleased to know that you are all right, also the children, 2 weeks today I shall be with you again, that's the day I am waiting for. It has rained most of today, but I got a good walk in first thing this morning before it clouded over. I have had a quiet day today, nothing much doing. Your letter was the high spot. I am sending cards to Ken and Jan (6)*, Miss Eyre and Harvey tomorrow if I can manage it. The Matron and Sisters are very nice to me and are*

most anxious that I should have all the facilities that are available. I can go to bed as early as I wish and have my supper brought to me if I let them know. There is very little to tell you tonight except that I love you more each day. I shall be thankful to get back home again, although I realise that my stay here may do me good.
All my love to you and the children, more tomorrow

Good night love

Harold

Room 40
Southport Conv H.
Seabanks Rd
Southport
11.30M
March 1/1938

Darling
Many thanks for your letter dated 5.0pm Monday. Very glad to know that you are all quite well and that you are getting some odd jobs done in the garden. I feel much better today, I am gradually getting more used to it and settling down, although the feeling of home sickness still persists. I have just had another massage, this time on the shoulder, it was very nice, but not really as effective as you do it, it is too short and too gentle, but I must be thankful for small mercies, with so many people to do. I had a charming letter from Harvey this morning and parcel of 4 packets of 20 Players (cigarettes) with no name but a request of my autograph, I'm almost sure it is one of Harvey's tricks.
The days don't seem nearly so long now that I have got over the first few days, I think that I shall be much more contented than I thought possible at first. The Sister and Matron are most helpful in all things and the latter has put me off eggs and substituted marmalade. By the way, the money question was quite in order, I had 15/- in my top pocket and I thought I only had 12/6. Peace of mind restored. I

think I shall go to one of the Picture Houses tomorrow afternoon, matinee performance if seats for 6d (sixpence) on production of 'Home' cmd. I am sending herewith the Doctor's certificate for NH purposes, we get them each Tuesday. The sun is very nice this morning but the wind is still too rough for me. I hope in a day or two to be able to get out and enjoy the sea air properly. 12.50 pm have just had a nice dinner, boiled fish, potatoes and cabbage, followed by rice pudding, 2 helpings of each. I'm just beginning to take an interest in food now. 2.0 pm, endeavouring to add to this letter, but thoughts do not come too readily on a full stomach, so I think I had better close and leave any further news until tomorrow.

Bless you my darling. This is another day nearer to when I return to you all.

Goodbye for now my darling
With all my love and kisses

Yours ever

Harold

Southport
Weds 1 o/c
2/3/ 1938

My Darling

Many thanks for your most welcome letter and those of the children. Very glad to know that you are all alright and keeping well. I am to have another massage and a deep pool bath tomorrow, so in my next letter I'll tell you all about it. I am beginning to get settled down now, so things don't bother me so much, but that doesn't imply that I don't want the next 8 days to go before I come home to you. Please don't bother to make any arrangements to fetch me before the time is up. As the days go by I shall feel happy reckoning up the days to come.

Sorry I forgot to enclose the medical certificate yesterday, but I must remember it today. We have just had dinner, tripe and sago (not together of course). I shall surprise you with my appetite when I get home. Did you see the children's letters? They are very sweet and quaint as one reflects upon their individual characters and the way they express themselves. I haven't sent those postcards yet. I want to do it today if I can. My thoughts will be with the class tomorrow night (Thursday). I hope Harvey will be able to be there to help. Today is quite fine, sunny up to now, although the wind is very boisterous. I went along the prom after breakfast but I had to shelter from it, it almost swept me off my feet. A lot of men are leaving tomorrow and about 90 more coming in. The place is always full right through the year. There are 470 here now.

Please give my love to the children, I will answer their letters in a few days. I have just written postcards to Ken and Jan, Misses Eyre, Roland Jackson, T. Baggott (7)*, Mr and Mrs G Richardson. It's a case of work fast while the tripe's in you.*

5.30pm have had a blow-out of stewed rhubarb and blancmange and I feel like sleeping it off now. It has remained fine today although the wind on the sea front is still too strong for me. This is one more day nearer home and you, my love, and then we shall be happy.

All my love and kisses my darling

Kiss the children for me and tell them I shall be glad to see them again

Goodnight sweetheart

Yours as ever

Harold

Southport
5.30pm Friday

Darling
Well, another day gone, and a beautiful day too. I had a lovely sea water bath this afternoon, with full supervision and every help possible even with dressing. And I've got my sling, it's a great improvement. Breakfast, bread and marmalade, dinner, boiled cod, haricot beans and potatoes, and rice pudding. Tea, jelly and custard. Supper, the inevitable bread and milk, still can't grumble, I've gained 4 lbs since I came. Carl Brisson (8) *came in here this afternoon to see one of the patients, there was a general scramble to see him and get his autographed photo, but I had been for a long walk and was too tired to bother to go out of the room. Many of the noisy element have got home and the new ones are not yet sufficiently settled to want to make whoopee. Thankyou, my love, for your loving thoughts and concentration last night. I didn't feel anything but I hardly expected to. It needs quiet and concentration before you can hope to feel any vibrations. I did write to Harvey about last Tuesday, but I had to send it home, as I was not sure where he was staying. I want to try to write to him tonight so that they get to him at home tomorrow. I want to remind him to write confirming the arrangements he made with the office the night we came. Just to make sure there is no hitch when it is time to come away. Everyday makes our reunion nearer, it doesn't seem nearly so far away now. So glad to hear that the children are all right and being good, and also that you are getting on well with your driving lessons. That will be a load off your mind. By the way, when I get home on Monday week, I want about half a sheep for my dinner, I've never seen a bit of mutton or lamb since I left home, with a stone of mashed potatoes, and either greens or peas, with an outsize pudding and poor Harvey discreetly toying with a piece of bread and jam. The post time is creeping on, so I must draw to a close*
With all my love
Ever yours

Harold

Southport
Thursday Mar 3/38
5.0pm

My Darling
Many Thanks for your letter received this morning. Delighted to hear that you are getting on so well with your driving lessons, hope you will not have any difficulty when you go for your test. That will be quite a load off your mind. Hope the children are all well and that they are being good for you and helping all they can. Please give Harvey my very kindest regards, and thanks for his many favours. I shall be concentrating on you all at 7.30 tonight wishing I was there in person. I wish you a very successful meeting, may it add greatly to your prestige. The weather has been lovely today, it's getting a bit cold now, but it has been very nice walking. I had another massage today, but with the new patients coming in he was not able to fix me up yet for my deep pool bath. I am having a sling tomorrow, also my water tested that is because I refused eggs on most occasions, so they want to test my nephritis. I shall be thinking of you sitting up until the small hours and poor little me fast asleep in my little bed. I sleep really well now and don't wake until they begin to stir about 5.30 in the morning. It is surprising to find me ready for my meals now. Bread and jam for breakfast. Rabbit, potatoes with rice pudding for dinner, bread and jam for tea and I suppose the usual bread and milk for supper. I haven't very much news to tell you tonight, the days seem to go very quickly just now, all to the good, I shall all the sooner be home again.
Please give my love to the children, my best wishes to Harvey and all my love and kind thoughts for you my sweetheart.
Ever Yours

Harold

Southport
March 6th 38
9.30am

My Dearest
Many Thanks for your letter of yesterday. Very glad you are keeping well, also the children. It was very nice of you to meditate on me last night (Thursday I mean) but owing to the lack of peace and quiet it was quite impossible for me to receive it. It was very nice of Mrs Baguly to bring the eggs, I hope they turn out alright and that the chicks do well. I had a very nice letter from Miss Eyre last night, a bookmark of Mr Finandoon's photo, and a number of cuttings from the 'American Theosophist", Miss Codd's monthly page mostly dealing with the inner life (3a)*. Sorry to hear that your Pa is not so well again. Regarding Walter Stretton* (9)*, I am not at all surprised, I guessed something of the kind would be happening sometime. Regarding my return, Harvey's suggestion will suit me very nicely, but what an awful day it will be for him, over 200 miles on what should be his rest day, it is him I am thinking of. I wouldn't like him to have to mollify Rene, if possible, in order to do me a very good turn. However, I will leave it entirely to you to fix up what you can because I know you will do the best you can under the circumstances. In any case I shall not ask permission to stay on until the Saturday morning. My arm is much more comfortable with the sling. Sample of urine shows a little albumin and no blood, so considering the addition of meat to my diet (but not here) that is quite good. The medical documentation after consisted of handing in my card, him telling me to take things easy and that was that. I am not sure if I told you that they weighed me on arrival. I pulled 8st 8 lb. I got on the scales a few days ago when I had to take the urine sample and I had put on 4 lbs. The weather is still very nice, although nights and mornings are quite chilly. Owing to the leg ache and general tiredness due to the strong air, I am not able to walk as far as often as I would like but I'm not doing too bad. I'm so sorry to know that you are not feeling too good, I hope that feeling will soon pass off. I'll cure that when I get home jolly quick. Interested to hear news from Mr Baggott. I had quite forgot that the bakery existed. Eggs must be cheap just now, boiled egg for breakfast again*

today which meant bread and marmalade for me about the fifth time this week. I didn't go into supper last night, not worth the trek right down to the dining hall for the pint of milk well-warmed, so went across the road and had Bovril and biscuits and slept much more satisfied in consequence. It doesn't seem so far off till Saturday, now that is less than a week. The sooner it goes the better, I shall be pleased. I'm getting awfully excited about it internally, just like a schoolboy going on his holiday. Scarcity of news makes it impossible to make this letter longer so I will close with all my love to you and the children

Ever yours for ever

Harold

PS I hope George (10) *is starting to get things planted.*

Southport
Tues Mar 8th 1938
11.0 am

Darling

Delighted to get your letter this morning. So sorry to hear that you have not been feeling very grand. Hope you are getting back to normal by now. I had a very nice letter from Harvey by the same post, he is calling for me on Friday afternoon about 4.0 pm, taking me to Bredbury and starting for Leicester about 11.0 or 12.0 arriving home about 4.0 or in time for tea, so that is something exciting to look forward to. Rene had her front teeth out yesterday so she won't be feeling very proud of herself for a little while. The report on the sample urine [stet sample of urine] was quite decent, some albumen, not much, and test for blood nil. I am having massage 3 times a week, very gentle and only lasts 10 minutes, but with having my arm in the sling it has gone very lazy and won't do a thing now, but I think the shoulder shows a little improvement. The reason that Harvey hadn't heard from me earlier was that I had been putting the wrong address, I put Arden Park Rd, instead of The Crescent, Arden Park. However I want to write to him today thanking him for the arrangements I told you about earlier in this letter. Glad you are looking forward to Saturday. I'm quite kittenish this morning and

keep smiling broadly to myself for no apparent reason, but I know what I'm smiling about. It's lovely to think that I shall be with you again in 4 days from now. After the racket here, I don't think I shall hear the children. I had a nice letter from Ken yesterday, started on Thursday midnight, continued on Friday and posted on Saturday. It was very kind of him to put the wire netting up in the orchard that is a good job done. I shall have to close now as it's getting near to dinner time and I'm due for massage just after.
All my love Sweetheart, keep smiling, it won't be long now.
Please give my love to the children and tell them I'm looking forward to seeing them.
Ever Yours

Harold

Southport
Weds March 9th 1938
3.30pm

Darling
I hope everything is alright with you all because I haven't had a letter today, and I wondered if all is well. I have just had my last sea water bath, as I've got to stop here in the test room for two hours. I get my massage at 3 o/c tomorrow for the last time and then it won't seem long until I see you. The weather is fine today but dull with a rather cold boisterous wind. Too cold to sit about. The one or two people with whom I have become rather pally are going home tomorrow and there is a dance in the concert hall tonight so it won't be any use going to bed early tonight. I don't know but I should judge it will be round about 5 o/c when we arrive home on Saturday. I hope you will be there to greet us in. I trust you will be feeling quite yourself by then. There is no news to tell you tonight. I shall be thinking of you all tomorrow (Thursday) at 7.30pm onwards. As Harvey won't be there to assist, I hope you carry it through alright. If there is any chance of getting anywhere quiet I am going to try and concentrate on you at the meeting today to see if I can get

anything through. I hope you will convey to Ken my sincere thanks for his most useful help whilst I have been away. Take care of the brooding hen and her eggs, mind the fox doesn't have chance to get near them. Must close now, as a number of the men are coming back from their two-hour walk.

All my love and wishes darling and, until Saturday, God bless you

Ever yours

Harold

A few weeks after his return home from Southport a second stroke led to Harold's death on July 3rd 1938, a year before the outbreak of the Second World War on September 2nd 1939. Elsie's father came to the house after Harold's death and asked to be able to attend the funeral. Because of an estrangement between them, Elsie wouldn't allow him to attend and Henry respected her wishes to stay away.

Harold, Elsie and Family

Above: Harold on his trip to the Isle of Wight to see the Schneider Trophy event. Below Elsie and left with one of her babies

Above: Peter left, and Tony, Below: Pamela with either Peter or Tony

Above: Elsie and Tony or Peter and Pamela
Below: Peter, Harold and Pamela

Left Peter at the seaside

Right: Pamela with Harold

Above: Tony and Peter

Above: Tony and Pamela feeding the deer in Bradgate Park

Above: Peter, Pamela and Tony

Pamela, Peter and Tony, on holiday at Elkstone in Derbyshire

Above left: Tony, Right: Peter

Above from left: Tony, Pamela and Peter

Above: Tony, Peter and Pamela
Below: Tony and Peter

Pamela, Peter and Tony in happier days before their father's death

Southport Convalescent Hospital, Seabanks Road, as it appears today

Elsie and Harold's dream home in Newtown Linford that became "Uranus", The Bradgate Guesthouse.

Harold is buried at All Saints Parish Church, Newtown Linford, Leicestershire

Part 3

Chapter 10
"The Guesthouse".

Elsie's journal describes how she came to turn their home into a guesthouse in the early days of her widowhood after Harold's death in the summer of 1938.

As well as the Theosophical Society, Elsie and Harold had been members of the 'Astrological Society' and a conservation society called 'The Friends of the Trees' or 'Men of The Trees'. Harold had planted or initiated the planting of a large orchard to the left of the house with a footpath that ran along the side. Tony has memories of having to treat the trees with creosote like substance to guard against disease.

Mrs Mossop had a sweet shop just down the road from the guesthouse and was married with a daughter. Her daughter lived a few doors down in a bungalow, and Elsie often sent overflow guests there to sleep; they would come back to the guesthouse for meals. The shop sometimes had Walls ice-cream for sale. Word would get round and everyone would rush to buy the rare treat which because it was war time it had to be signed for.

Cyril Pamphilon was a friend of Harold and Elsie and had helped with the design of the house. Alma, Elsie's niece has memories of an upstairs roof space being used for star gazing with telescopes. There are conflicting stories of whether this was at Newtown Linford or Thornton where Elsie and Cyril later moved to. If it was Newtown this no doubt all changed after Harold's death when the upstairs would have been needed for extra bedrooms for the guesthouse.

After Harold's death and while running the guesthouse Elsie supplemented her widow's pension by writing a booklet called 'Lady Jane Grey of Bradgate Park'. These were sold to her guests and visitors to the park. The booklet was kept on a table in the guesthouse hall. The children were sometimes required to sell homemade lemonade and juice at the bottom of the drive and the booklets would appear on the table as well. A slightly later version of the booklet can be seen in Appendix D.

Memories of The Bradgate Guesthouse by Elsie May Pamphilon, formerly Hartell.

The following list of guests and stories are about people who stayed with Elsie's at her guesthouse in Newtown Linford, Leicestershire. She named the house 'Uranus' after the astrological sign.

The Hewits (Jewellers)

The wards 4 honeymoons

The people from Romania – Hitler

The deaf lady, the teasing girls, had breakfast in bed

The Lady who came, she told me to keep out of the servants' way while spring cleaning was done.

The naughty soldier boys who tried for bed and breakfast with their girl pick-ups.

The Officer who with a lady missed the bus, who was exposed

The lesbian lady – a clergyman's wife and friend

The clergyman who constantly quarreled with his wife

The man and wife preachers with the appalling children who competed, with the aid of spoon and soup to make the biggest splash on the newly decorated ceiling and must not be corrected because this was psychologically bad for them.

The other child, who persisted in sitting on top of the piano with her feet on the keys. Modern mums at this time were adopting the cult of no discipline for children. This poor mum committed suicide a fortnight after her stay.

The one I like to think of is the dear old soul, a widow.

In the thirties just prior to the onset of war I quite suddenly became a widowed mother of three young children. We had recently built a rather large bungalow in a well known Leicestershire beauty spot. I had some money, not very much, but the house was paid for. My only income was twenty one shillings pension from the government. I had to earn some money somehow, well meaning friends suggested I should sell the house and buy a cheaper one, and that it was economic suicide to even think of keeping the car. Intuition told me however, to give myself a month to get over the shock and to think. I knew from the start that only as a last resort would I take any job that would cause me to leave the children too much alone, their loss was as great as mine and would be doubly so if I were away from them.

About a week later I was driving into Leicester when I saw an elderly lady struggling on foot up an incline ahead of me. I was feeling utterly wretched and thought I just can't pick her up, I don't want to talk to anyone, but when I did get level with her I stopped and offered her a lift. I didn't know her, I had only been in the village about a year, so when she had settled down and thanked me, she said, "Do you live around here?" Still not wanting to talk I just answered "Yes". She looked hard at me and said "I thought I knew everyone around here" then as if remembering something she said "Are you that young woman who lost her husband last week?" I answered that I was. She then said "Are you going to be alright me duck, I mean with three little children to keep?" I said "I suppose so". Her reply was "you could make a good living in the house you know. I cater for teas in the village and I'm always being asked if I will take people in for holidays. I could send you dozens of people". I said I couldn't think of it, we had planned and dreamed about this house in which we had hoped to be so happy. She got out of the car when she reached her destination then putting her head through the window said, "Think about it me duck, and let me know". I did my business in town returning in the late afternoon, to find on my doorstep a lady and three children, they had been sent by my friend of the morning.

Would I please consider taking into my home the children whose mother had to have a serious operation in a week's time, their aunt was a business woman and the children would be home from school for the August holiday. My heart went out to them when I learned that their father had died seven months before. These three children were my first guests, their mother convalesced with me and we became good friends.

Literally hundreds of people stayed in my house during the years that followed. The war started and finished and still they came. I think the children resented it a little at times but they were reasonable and didn't seem to be hurt in any way by this invasion into their home, in fact they got much fun out of it all at times, as when, for instance, we had a couple staying who were vegetarians of a very extreme kind who lived mainly on raw foods. They had a small terrier dog and were constantly telling people that the dog was vegetarian too; the children knew that the dog should be carnivorous so they saved their own portion of meat, which was generous of them considering it was war time - and gave it to the dog. The animal just relished it and followed them everywhere, much to the owner's surprise.

I visited a relative in the local hospital. In a bed opposite was a young man who was very ill, not expected to recover. My relative called to him telling him where I came from and I went over to talk to him. He told me that he and his fiancé often came that way and that when he was better they would marry and had decided to honeymoon there - there was a war on and people couldn't travel far. I said, more to console him than anything else, "Hurry up and get better and you shall stay in my guesthouse". He did get better; he spent his honeymoon with me as did also three of his brothers. My name spread far and wide among the boys in the forces as a happy place to spend a honeymoon. Many of them never came back. I am glad to have been of service to them.

In 1938 we had visitors who had lived in Romania but had come away with their four children and were hoping to settle down in England. They were English. I asked why they had given up good circumstances they had enjoyed to come to England where things were far from good. They answered that Hitler meant war and that as soon as he had his 1939 harvest in, it would come; it did, and what a surprise it was to us all. Their small boy of seven who spoke several languages, when asked which he preferred, said, "English of course, but it's more important to know German".

There was the officer who missed the last bus and I, taking the lady with him to be his wife, offered them a double room with two single beds; at breakfast the next morning the girl was spotted by one of the other guests as a buyer in a local store rumoured to be unmarried. This was soon broadcast among the other guests and commented about often, much to the embarrassment of the couple, to say nothing of myself.

There was the elderly officer who came every 4th week-end and whose supposed wife joined him; he was as solicitous as a bridegroom and we heard wonderful tales of their life together; one day I called to see a friend in the office in which she worked and here was my officer's wife, she was a single woman and my friend had known her for twenty years.

There was the clergyman who constantly quarreled with his wife, much to the embarrassment of all present.

The husband and wife Baptist Ministers with 2 children, who were never corrected because this was psychologically bad for them. Their chief delight was in flipping soup with a spoon to try to splash the newly decorated ceiling and walls.

There was another child who would sit on the top of the piano and dig her heels into the front panel. This one's mother believed in the cult that never corrected or said "No" to a child, it was rife about then. She, poor woman took her own life two weeks later.

Two ladies turned up one Monday morning, having previously booked by phone, in a chauffer driven Rolls Royce. I gathered on the phone that they were Author and Secretary, they had been with me for about a week when the family of one of them descended upon me and told me that the elder one had left her husband, a clergyman, and that they had come to try to break up this lesbian relationship. They didn't succeed, but my knowledge of life was expanding.

The one I like to think of was a dear old lady of 84 with a grown up mentally deficient daughter. One lovely summer evening I persuaded a friend of hers who was visiting to stay with the daughter while I used a little of my precious petrol to take her for a run in Charnwood Forest. I didn't know that she had ever been there before. The sun was setting and seemed to bowl along quite low as I drove slowly along the almost deserted road. With tears in her eyes she said "May we stop here, please?" I thought she was overcome by the beauty of the scene and sat quite still and didn't speak. Some minutes later she said' "Thank you, my dear, you have given me my happiest moment for 55 years, it was in this lane on a stile where that gate is that my husband proposed to me. We were on a Sunday school outing, both teachers. A few weeks later I read of her death in a local paper.

This, then, was some of my experience as a widow. It was hard work. I didn't make a fortune but I did manage to make a living for my children. I learned a good deal about people and made many friends.

Part 4

Letters to Elsie May Hartell from Cyril Pamphilon 1940 to 1945

Cyril Pamphilon (1903-1971) and Elsie

Cyrils Letters

Chapter 11

The 'San', Theosophy, Difficult Relationships, Lessons to be Learnt, Rupert Brooke, Colin and Elna

Cyril Ellis Pamphilon was born on August 24th 1903. He refers to himself as 'my cockney self' in one of his letters and his birth record reveals that he was born in Edmonton, Dagenham and Baptised in Haringey, London. Family history suggests that Cyril was of Greek Orthodox origin and his letter of 21st May 1940 would seem to support this. His Greek surname means "loved by all". Cyril lived in Peterborough as an adult before his marriage to Elsie. By profession Cyril was an architectural draughtsman, and used his skills to assist Harold and Elsie with the design of their Newtown Linford home. He worked at Constone Limited which was opposite to South Wigston High School where Alma, Elsie's niece was a pupil. She remembers him waving to her often when he was coming from and going to work and she was on the school bus. Cyril was also a keen club cyclist. "Aunt and Uncle" at Healing *(near Grimsby in Lincolnshire)* were Cyril's relatives and Colin and Elna were his brother and sister.

Through his letters it appears that Cyril also belonged to the 'Theosophical Society' and is probably how he met Elsie and Harold. Some of his references to the 'learned people' and the publications mentioned appear to be connected with the society. The Theosophical Society studies various religions, such as Buddhism and Hinduism but imposes no belief system on its members. Harvey, a member of the society, also featured prominently in Cyril's letters but in a much more negative way than he did in Harold's.

Most of Cyril's letters to Elsie were written from Markfield Sanatorium (11) where he was recovering from tuberculosis (TB). TB patients were often resident for up to two years for treatment until medication became more available. The main treatment was bed rest, good food grown on the hospital farm and fresh air. Patients were exposed to the air including the winter air and snow. Medical treatment for Cyril would probably have included streptomycin injections, air treatment for the lungs, gentle exercise and bed rest. The hospital radio that Cyril refers to was called "Sangram", and shows were put on for patients by the Markfield Dramatic Society. Visiting hours were two hours only on Wednesdays, Saturdays and Sundays (Markfield Local History Group 2006).

Cyril was very proud of the fact that he was considered to have been the first person to have been cured of TB because he was such a good patient. It is unknown if he was the first to be cured at the Sanatorium, or in the county.

The sanatorium became Markfield Court, a residential home for elderly people, until it closed down in 2017.

To Mrs E.M. Hartell
"Uranus"
The Bradgate Guest House
Anstey Road
Newtown Linford
Nr Leicester

Markfield
Sunday 31/3/40

Elsiemay dear
I really must drop you a line so soon after your visit this afternoon to say how very deeply sorry I am and amazed too, at the terrible treatment you have experienced and suffered at the hands of those you had thought to be friends.
You know that I am not at all perturbed (only annoyed) that they should embellish my apparent evil doings and the misfortune of my health, but I am more than sorry that the most happy friendship I have had with you should have to come under the fire of the enemy and that you have to bear the brunt of it all while I am away from it.
I still cannot think why Sam (13) *should be so unkind and dishonourable to you after all the help you have given him. I sincerely hope that one day he will realize and will be man enough to apologise and thank you for all your kindness and friendship.*
For the others, there is no excuse. They are old enough to know better and deserve real punishment for a cowardly betrayal of friendships ... and to think, Elsie, that you have opened your house to them as a haven from all their troubles and for free discussion. Of what use is the study of theosophy and learned treatises on occult subjects when the sacred name of friendships is so easily desecrated.
As for their presumption about your morals, that privilege is only allowed to them after they have put their own house in order.
You know my sentiments about morals Elsie, and that I am only disgusted with the ignorance of so called cultured people who are supposed to know what constitutes the art of living fully. That sex should confuse and baffle these learned ones amazes me, and then to mix this up with morality and morals, well, 'I asks yer' to quote my cockney self.

I was so glad to see you again and it is very sweet of you to make the journey, especially as it is so difficult for you to get away. I am looking forward to the time when I can visit you again for a real chat 'for old time's sake'.
I am so glad to hear you had a jolly time at the dance, it would be a lovely break for you from domestic duties etc. It was my firm's staff dance last Friday. I haven't heard from home during the past weeks so hope no news is good news. Expect Colin (14) *will have been called up by now.*
Dorothy Diken was married on Easter Saturday and spent the honeymoon in Stratford cum Broadway district. She is now a Mrs Jones and will live at Ormskirk, Lancs.
I guess the gang (15) *will have played some April 1st tricks upon you. Mrs B. said how much they had grown so I expect you will have to label them for me to recognise them.*
I hope I didn't shock Mrs Fabrielle too much about shooting the nurses at Markfield. I was surprised to see her walk in with you.
I do thank you Elsie for the kind gifts for my tea. I do enjoy my food these days especially now that I am able to go to the dining hall where it is served up so much nicer.
It's great to think of the coming spring days and I have appreciated so much this year the flowers typical of spring. In spite of man's inhumanity to man there are, as Rupert Brooke (16) *said, 'the eternals, the good, the lovely and the true' and perhaps spring of all seasons indicates a basic principle from which come the experiences of beautiful things like colour , music and form etc.*
I do hope the spring will bring you much happier conditions and truer friends and a greater confidence in the knowledge that all the good and the happiness you have given to others is an addition to these things which never die.
My love and good wishes are always with you and I trust you will be able to get some rest after your busy and very trying time and that your neuralgia pains have disappeared.
Yours very affectionately

Cyril

To Mrs E.M. Hartell
"Uranus"
The Bradgate Guest House
Newtown Linford
Nr Leicester

Markfield
7/4/40

Elsie dear
What a lovely evening it turned out to be after you had gone. I went to the church service at 5.00pm and thought of you in my meditations and prayers.

It was indeed great to see, this afternoon, that Elsie which I admire and love emerging almost unscathed from the heavy blows and trials which the past month or two you have had to bear. So please accept my very sincere congratulations on your achievement.

I agree with you that as in all trials there are many lessons to be learnt and it will be a great victory if you remain unattached to the event caused by the weakness of character in those who have been foolish enough to endeavour to destroy and dishonour their relationships with you. From it, too, one can see the value of discrimination and judgment in our relationships so that we shall be on our guard against exposing sacred things to those who only desecrate them.

I am indeed sorry that you have lost these friends but it is best that it should be so until they are strong and able enough to value and appreciate the honour of your kindness to them. I am so glad for your sake that past events have clarified the outlook for you, but feel with you the pain of it all, and rejoice with you that the things that matter in the long run remain and are imperishable and those who really love you, in the true understanding of comradeship, are with you.

There are many things which they have said or implied which one can get a laugh out of, such as our notorious trips to our country seat etc. But the incident of the deed box must always leave a very nasty taste. Undoubtedly the Rt Hon. Harvey was very peeved that you did not play into his hands so did not have any scruples as to which methods he used to attain his end. But he had met more than the ordinary type of woman so was in the end easily outplayed.

I forgot to convey to you my mother's and sisters and also aunt and uncle at Healing good wishes to you. Also to tell you that Howard (17) *and Mr Frearson are visiting me next Sunday but of course don't let that prevent you coming if you so wish and circs* (18) *allow.*

Elsie it is really grand to feel my strength coming back again and although I still have much to regain I am conscious of a steady improvement in whatever I attempt. But I don't know quite how I shall manage without my Charnwood air when I get back into the outside world again. I shall have to bring a supply with me. Like 'Bass' it's great stuff and at the moment seems almost indispensible to me.

I am very pleased to learn that you hope to be able to peruse the lectures again. They are really worth more than their weight in gold, at every stage of the great journey, and are the keys to the storehouse of every kind of knowledge.

I hope you will be able to have some hours of quiet and rest amidst the activity of the everyday world, also joyous times in jolly and interesting company.

You know my wishes are always for your happiness and advancement and I do appreciate the help you have given me at all times and the joy of your company.

Very kind regards to 'the gang' and to all friends I know, i.e. Ken and Jan etc

Ever my love Elsie dear

Affectionately Yours

Cyril

To Mrs E.M. Hartell
"Uranus"
The Bradgate Guest House,
Newtown Linford
Nr Leicester

Markfield
Tuesday
Post Mark April 1940

My dear Elsie
It gave me much happiness to know and sense that you are feeling much happier in yourself, and that with spring, the blue skies are returning again to Uranus and you.
I agree with your policy of leaving the persons and events of the immediate past to themselves for disintegration of all that has been so unhappy and disrupting and to hold fast to the experience and lessons learnt.
I have smiled since about the 'Will' episode and have been amazed at the audacity of it all. They say 'cheek will get you through'. It is so difficult to understand why a person younger in years and experience of the world should have the bad manners to behave as though he was your great grandfather. I have always doubted the great man's knowledge of things from scraps of conversation with him. He is well below now in character because even the simple things of life are beyond his control and use.
Thank you so much for coming up on Sunday even though I had visitors. I am afraid Howard didn't look too fit after his rough time during the winter. I expect you would notice a difference as you remarked upon it.
I had a letter from Peterboro' yesterday and Elna (19) *says she and mother are not doing very well as yet. I expect a holiday is required to put them right.*
Colin goes to Salisbury Plain on Thurs, they have drafted him to the Royal Artillery so he is rather disappointed at not getting into the R.A.F. as a Radio Mechanic.
My cubicle looks very bright and cheery now that we have flowers which we have arranged as tastefully as the masculine brain and hands can be expected to do in such things.

I hope you enjoyed the film 'Escape to Happiness' if you were able to see it and that Leslie Howard regained his reputation by portraying the more idealist type of character. I hope the new Swedish star Ingrid Bergman was as beautiful and charming as the majority of her countrywomen.
The head doctor has now returned and on Monday gave me 10 hrs up so have all my meals in the dining hall and the next move will be a walk to the san gates. I smiled at Howard's suggestion that I ought to remain at the san much longer. I certainly agree on principle but it's only human to wish to be amongst friends etc as soon as possible. But, in any case, I shall take the doctor's advice as to when I should leave.
Hoping this finds you in the 'pink' and all at Uranus.
Happy thoughts my dear, and a smile.
Always my love Elsie

Very affectionately yours

Cyril

To Mrs E.M. Hartell
"Uranus"
The Bradgate Guest House
Newtown Linford
Nr Leicester

Markfield
Thursday
Post mark 18/4/40

Elsie Dear
Your letter to hand this morning, for which many thanks.
Re coupons; should be pleased to have some only on condition that it will give you no inconvenience whatever as my requirements so far are relatively unimportant, but if the coupons are really begging then I can use them as a reserve for the time when I can utilize the car which I hope will be the near future. Have learnt today that I may have to go into a hut (12) *about Saturday, regret leaving my present*

cubicle. But there are three going home on Saturday and so three huts will be vacant by then.
Hope you had a jolly interesting time at the 'flicks'.
Must say cheeribye now, in order to catch post.
Keep smiling my dear
My love
Yours always

Cyril

To Mrs E.M. Hartell
"Uranus"
The Bradgate Guest House,
Newtown Linford
Nr Leicester

Markfield
Monday
Post Mark 23 April 1940

Elsie dear
I regret that your visit had such an abrupt ending on Sunday. Apparently I was the last victim of the Sister's onslaught, as when I arrived at the dining hall all the lads with visitors had been ticked off; so they were ready to pull my leg when I appeared. However, you will be interested to learn that I went to Church afterwards and was condoned for all my sins of omission and commission!!?
Here's a <u>big</u> thank you for the joy of your company and all the kindly gifts to gladden the tummy of man, also for the ration coupons which will give me an initial advantage when I leave the San.
Did I tell you (I don't think I did) that my mother and Elna have gone to Guildford for a week or ten days, so I hope the change will be a turning point in their health. My bother is now at Devizes.
Now that I have graduated to a hut I feel quite cut off from all those rough lads on the ward and instead feel like a hermit.
If you have any artistic pictures or statues you don't want they will be most appropriately welcomed to console my feeling of loneliness.

Elsie it's great to know that you are again back to the strength of your own peace. I am glad too that you have been able to contact again the lectures and I am sure that the trials and pain of recent experiences will have enabled you to view the teachings and counsels in another light and to obtain from them greater vision, understanding and strength. The lecture "The Integral Purpose" has been of immense help to me. Service is dealt with in a most practical manner and yet the dignity of service is not robbed of any altruistic motive or purpose and so the balance is maintained in all relationships.

The other day I had an enquiry from U.O. Headquarters as to whether I should be able to attend a summer retreat if they are able to arrange such a treat.

Can hear the tune "Smiling thro" being played over the wireless as I write – so send you a smile too. Sincere good wishes for your happiness and my love and affection as always

Yours

Cyril

To Mrs E.M. Hartell
"Uranus"
The Bradgate Guest House
Newtown Linford
Nr Leicester

Markfield
Monday evening
(Spring, no date)

Elsie dear

It seems that the weather has switched back to November today, but what a lovely day you brought yesterday so mustn't grumble. And the countryside has been so wonderfully charming the last fortnight. And the spring flowers this year seem extra refreshing and thrillingly beautiful.

Once again as I write, the air "Smiling thro" is coming over the wireless so it must be our signature tune.

I heard from my sister that she and mother had been to Guildford for a week and that the change had made them both feel much better. They sent a box of fruit from dear old Surrey.

I haven't heard from Colin but expect to get a line as soon as he gets settled down to routine. I guess he will feel it very strange at first as he hasn't been a wanderer from home like yours truly, which has been a complaint with me since I was about 5-ish but modern youth has plenty of confidence and so it should stand them well in the Army, else get them shot.

I am pleased to say the coupons are quite O.K. and George (the garage man) will fill me up at the time I need the car. I really had not expected any difficulty as George and I are good pals.

In my opinion you are very wise in stopping, completely, relationships with all of the mischief-makers. Although I believe that we must be always ready to forgive and be forgiven, but only if reconciliation is truly sincere on both sides. But in this case your interests are at the mercy of the unscrupulous.

Regarding their accusations re Sam and yourself it's just another example of their childishness and feebleness of character. All of them without exception have some sex problem, fear or inhibition of their own and so their outlook is therebye crooked and biased accordingly. You have such a finely balanced outlook and knowledge of all matters appertaining to sex, whereas their view is coloured by a sordid outlook, which unfortunately is so commonplace today in all sections of society. I and anyone who really knows you would never dream or imagine anything so 'un Elsie-like'. Like Syd Walker, you do meet some strange 'how do's', the hospital episode was certainly one. I hope everything turned out O.K. and that the suitor of your sweet seventeen period had his affair straightened out.

Pam's wee bowl of primroses look very charming indeed, for which my very grateful thanks for her kind thoughts and labour.

In closing I send you happy thoughts, grateful thanks for so very, very much.

Yours in all that is good, beautiful and true
Ever my love dear
Affectionately yours

Cyril

To Mrs E.M. Hartell
"Uranus"
The Bradgate Guest House
Newtown Linford
Nr Leicester

Markfield
6/5/40

Elsie my dear

It was great to see you on Sunday feeling and looking that 'youe de sure' typical of sweet seventeen, although 'anno domini' has added another unit in terms of time.

I must confess I had suspected that you would not be able to come along owing to pressure of business, especially as the weather was such that many would be out and about in Newtown ready to give you a call.

Once again I attended the evening service at the wee church and your vicar officiated and you were much in my thoughts and prayers.

I must sincerely thank you for your kind gifts; the violets look very fresh and lively on my locker.
Thank you also for very, very kindly putting your time and assistance in conveying me to Croft when I am due to return.
So far it appears that I shall remain here a few weeks longer, so, I hope by so doing I shall avoid your extra 'rushy' period and so give you the minimum of inconvenience in leaving 'Uranus'.
Have had a letter from Elna to-day and she and mother appear to be much better and have news also of Colin who seems to have settled down fairly well and so far is attached to the anti aircraft section of the Royal Artillery. He says that his chief difficulty so far is getting used to heavy boots after being accustomed to light shoes in civilian life.
I was interested in your mention of the theosophist's daughter, it appears most difficult to advise as apparently the young lady is aware of the type she is associating with and willingly follows them and finds their company satisfying to her outlook on life.
Sexual perversion seems to be very common these days in most countries and is a definite social problem.
You will certainly be able to write an interesting book one of these days and have bumped into many strange people.
Will close in order to catch post. Please give my kind regards to Ken and Jan when you see them, and to the gang.
Happy landings, and jolly thoughts. Hoping that Whitsuntide will bring you jolly guests, and interesting experiences.
May life and health and strength be with you
Ever my love, Elsie, and much affection

Yours in the master's service

Cyril

To Mrs E.M. Hartell
"Uranus", The Bradgate Guest House
Newtown Linford
Nr Leicester

Markfield
16/5/40

Elsie dear
It was a very pleasant surprise to see you on the Monday and to see Pam too. I hope her return journey was without any misadventures or directions etc. The blossoms do look fine and after I had put them in water they revived like magic.
I guess you will be looking forward to a break from a weekend of hectic activity and I hope you have been able to have some interesting interludes.
We had a whist drive for all up patients from all the wards on Tuesday evening and I assisted the M.C. etc as I always dodge cards if I can, without causing any unsociable feeling. So I was amongst the nurses and women patients so had to put my shyness on one side for the occasion. There are some smart girls, victims of the complaint – it seems such a pity that they should be so – but we also have some fine fellows on our ward that are so handicapped. Isn't life strange?
I took a walk to bluebell wood off the Newtown Lane on Tuesday afternoon. It was a fine sight indeed to see the blue haze over the ground and I also saw the Yeomanry memorial in Bradgate Park.
I expect you will become more active in your war duties now that the war is approaching our doorstep. I expect Italy to enter any moment, although many seem to think they will remain neutral.
Here's a cheeribye and a smile and grateful thanks for so many kindnesses.
My love to you, Elsie, and the gang
Very sincerely and affectionately yours

Cyril

PS. Had a line from Dolly P. Has started farming again at Sheepey. Dick has measles (not German)

To Mrs E.M. Hartell
"Uranus" The Bradgate Guest House,
Newtown Linford
Nr Leicester

The San Markfield
21/5/40

Elsie Dear

Your letter to hand this morning, for which many, many thanks. I missed your visit on Sunday, but of course did not expect you as I realised that with such lovely weather etc you would have heaps of callers, all to be attended to, making it almost a physical impossibility to leave. I am so glad that you are being so well patronaged, that everything has been so jolly and interesting. It is good that Pam and Joan have been so helpful and the hatching of the wee chicks more than thrilling for Pam.

I had a pleasant surprise on Saturday when my mother and Elna came over to see me. They would enjoy the outing very much because the weather was so lovely and the countryside so 'freshly' beautiful. Although they both showed signs of the strain etc. of the past months I was pleased to find them looking much better than I had anticipated, and on the mend, even though very slowly. They said Colin had been transferred to transport and that he had had a bad cough etc. so I guess the new rougher life is having some reaction, but I hope that in the long run it will be the best for health, although one cannot hope for too much from the Army, at least during war time.

I was very sorry to learn from your previous letter that Ruby had been on the war path again. Apparently she delights in maintaining the circulation of so much rubbish of no import. It is terribly 'childish' for one supposed to have reached the age of 14 and beyond. I regret that you should have to contact this all over again. Life is too full to have to include such distractions for long at a time.

I went to church again on Sunday. We had no organist so you can imagine your vicar endeavouring to lead in the hymns. However, in spite of such limitations I found the service helpful. The vicar spoke about the Trinity. You can imagine how I enjoyed considering the church orthodox view again and my relating it to that taught in the Ancient Wisdom (3b).

I too have admired so much the lovely spring evenings and nights and the moon has been grand and romantic: You were favoured to have the opportunity of sleeping under such a panoply of so much beauty. Yes I can imagine the charm of Bradgate from your garden. I had the joy of seeing it from afar last Sunday morning when I took a walk across the fields and came to a high spot from which dear old Bradgate could be seen. Naturally you and Uranus were always in my thoughts at that time.

I am pleased to say that my X-Ray yesterday (Mon) gave good results and the collapse (lung) is apparently still behaving O.K. for which I am truly thankful. At the time of writing have no information as to when I shall be leaving.

Please convey my greetings to Pam and the gang and all friends. My mother and sister and Mrs B send very kind regards.

Isn't the green of the countryside perfect just now? As it is the season of birth and tenderness it seems the very opposite to war and destruction.

So cheerybye dear one. Keep smiling through and every good wish for your welfare and may you have jolly interesting company and friends. Ever my warmest love and affection

Yours

Cyril

Chapter 12
Recovery, Germany, War Reflections and Duties, Astrology, the Wonder of Nature, and 'The Gang'.

In these letters in the early 1940's Cyril was recovering significantly and coming to the end of his time at Markfield Sanatorium. He expressed concern about war related activity that was occurring in Europe. Rationing would have been in force and a shortage of fresh food produce was evident. The 'Saving is Simple' stamp below was attached to one of Cyril's letters. Despite difficult times he was still able to contemplate, reflect on, and appreciate the wonder of nature. Elsie was continuing to pursue her astrological interests.

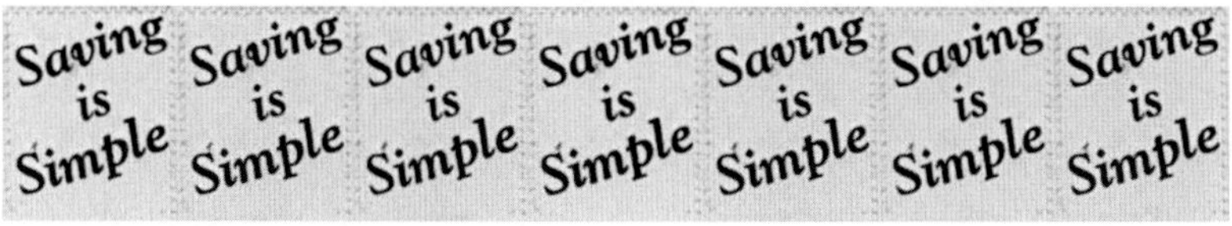

To Mrs E.M. Hartell
"Uranus"
The Bradgate Guest House
Newtown Linford
Nr Leicester

Markfield San
Tues
(Date not visible on postmark but early June as after Whitsun)

My dear Elsie

It was great to see you on Sunday and you must have the secret of youth to look so fresh after such a very busy fortnight.
Many, many thanks for the oranges which are very valuable to me now that I do not get much fresh salads etc. and I eat two oranges every day to help maintain the balance of protective foods.
I am pleased to report that the head doctor has put me on full walks so can now do about 5 miles – yesterday I did the full course and was amazed that even the hilly bits didn't make me puff even with only one lung to do the service of two, and my legs and self not at all fatigued, so there's hopes of rearing the lad.
Although I had hoped to have been out of the san for Whitsun – yet now I am pleased that I have continued to the end of the treatment as I am feeling much better for it, much as I would like to be out and doing something.
Howard has written to say that he is coming to see me on Sunday, probably with Mrs Frearson.
Phoebe wrote this week. She says she is much better in health and is helping at a nearby military hospital writing letters etc. for the soldiers.
Have also had Dorothy's wedding photograph which I will show you as she does look really charming in my opinion – but, of course, I am not an expert on such matters.
The international situation looks very, very grave now and our nation will have a severe trial of endurance and courage to face. It is

amazing to think how all the nations in Europe have calmly watched Germany build such a powerful and efficient war machine. Their faith in thoughts of peace and neutrality have not helped in any way as a preventative to the ultimate terror and brutality.

I think the idea of last Sunday being a day of prayer was a good one – it may appear hypocritical to turn to the source of all things in difficult times etc - but so often along the journey we have to be 'brought back' by such means.

Friday will be a year by the day since Irene died. So much has happened since that day of parting; many of the events have been the source of unhappiness and discord, whereas my sister seemed always to convey the calmer and more peaceful things of life by her manner and presence.

I expect your large family will have been reduced a little by now, giving you a little respite, but guess the pace will quicken again by the weekend.

Am going to a concert on Weds evening so will go all gay for a few hours, just like an excited youngster.

Will close with a smile and happy thoughts for your welfare, and the gang.

Ever sincerely my love Elsie
Warm affection

Yours Cyril

PS. Enclose 1 1/2 [one and a half] stamp with much thanks for petrol (1d cost and 1/2d carriage and overheads)

To Mrs E.M. Hartell
"Uranus"
The Bradgate Guest House
Newtown Linford
Nr Leicester

Markfield
Weds
(Early June after Whitson)

My Dear Elsie
Just a wee note to thank you for your kindness in looking after and bringing Eric over to see me, as I know how very very busy you are and every minute is precious and not easily spared from looking after your big family etc etc.
It was good to see Eric and the time went all too rapidly to make any except a few enquiries of all the many people whom I know in Eric's circle.
I trust Eric was not too exhausted by missing his meal. But I have a sincere 'fellow feeling' if he was missing a nice cup of tea.
Elsie, the beauty and tranquility which is expressed by the countryside at this time is such a vivid contrast to humanity's political and social troubles and discords, but we must not forget that Mother Nature can also have very wild and chaotic moods; such is the evolutionary process.
Although one has forecasted in mind much of what would happen in this war, yet the events have moved with such rapidity that it is difficult to adjust the situation before another is presented, and most of it seems too terrible to contemplate in all its confusion.
It is strange as since I told you my medical exam is due a week on Monday, it has now been brought back to next Monday, so I may hear something the following Thursday.
Well Cheeribye dear, keep smiling and every happy thought.
Ever my love Elsie
Affectionately Yours

Cyril
PS. To the gang, good hunting, and happy landings.

To Mrs E.M. Hartell
The Bradgate Guest House
Newtown Linford
Nr Leicester

The San Markfield
5/6/40

Elsie dear

Many, many thanks for your last two letters. It was awfully good of you to drop a line to my mother and Elna and I am sure they would appreciate your kindness at such a time.

How supremely grand is the weather. It should put everyone in good spirits even though outer activities are so distressing. One of the benefits of a sojourn in a san is the opportunity it gives to see and contemplate the inexhaustible wonder and beauty of nature in its varying moods, as the rush of outside activities does tend to shut out its sights and sounds.

I guess, dear, you will have had another hectic week and weekend and I trust you have been able to contact some very interesting people in consequence. I missed your visit on Sunday of course. I had a male visiting weekend. On Sat Mr Baker came in place of Mrs B. who was too unwell to make the journey. While on Sunday Howard brought Alan Pointon in place of Mrs Frearson who was on duty at the school for A.R.P. (20) *so you will realise I missed the 'feminine touch' and had to fall back on the nurses for consolation!!*

Did I tell you I am now on full walks and top grade, so have completed the course as far as the san is concerned, so may hear of my discharge anytime now.

Have been reading a book called ' Madame Chair' and have put it on one side for you as I think you would find some mental relaxation from its pages as it is light reading, yet with the power to take one for a mental holiday.

This morning I received a letter from Gracie and she enclosed details for the horoscope of her friend which I mentioned to you some time ago and she also asked if you would set up one for her also. I expect the present is more than out of the question for you to deal with them but let me know if and when you are able to deal with them so that I can acquaint Gracie accordingly.

The particulars are:-

Grace Ball born April 18th 1903 5am approx
Vera Harman born Nov 10th 1901 midnight approx

I believe that is all you require, if not, please let me know.
I wonder if you have been sleeping under the stars again, as the nights have been wonderfully superb for such 'openairishness' and it would be a lovely tonic after the rush of the daily round.
Will close now Elsie, as the post is due. So happy thoughts dear, and most grateful thanks for every helpful thought and deed.
With my love and affection Elsie
Yours as always

Cyril

Chapter 13
Leaving 'The San', Bradgate, Fred Astaire and Ginger Rogers, George Formby and Honeymoon Couples

Some of Cyril's letters were written from Croft in Leicestershire where he lived after leaving the sanatorium. Part of his subsequent convalescence was spent at Elsie's guesthouse, initially in a large shed at the side of the house called 'The Bungalow' which had electricity but no water supply. Jugs of water were fetched from the main house for him.

Many people stayed at the guesthouse, as detailed in Elsie's journal. Some are referred to in Cyril's letters, for example the 'honeymoon couples' and many others such as Joan Stretton and Sam seemed to come and go, helping out, supporting and adding to the life, busyness and vibrancy of the home.

There is a gap between Cyril's letter of October 1940 and August 1945. Elsie and Cyril married on 30th January 1941 at Leicester Register Office when she was 41 and he was 37. Their marriage certificate proves that Elsie was 41 years in 1941 and that her age at her first marriage to Harold was 18 and not 21. Pam, Peter and Tony were unaware of Elsie and Cyril's wedding plans until the day they were all gathered in the kitchen of the guesthouse one afternoon. Their mother and Cyril came in and announced that they had married that morning.

Cyril was a kindly, gentle and shy man. Peter, who would have been 12 years old when his mother remarried, always resented Cyril who he felt tried to replace his father. Although in later life Peter often said that Cyril was a lovely man, he just couldn't take to him as a teenage boy who had lost his father 3 years earlier.

At the guesthouse in the evenings, Cyril would often make a large saucepan of coffee; guests would gather in the lounge and encourage Elsie to talk to them about the many subjects which interested her, which she loved. Afternoon teas were often served in the garden at the guesthouse and Joan and Alma, Elsie's nieces, helped to serve the guests. Elsie and Cyril were both attached to All Saints Anglican Church in Newtown Linford.

To Mrs E.M. Hartell
"Uranus"
The Bradgate Guest House
Newtown Linford
Nr Leicester

3 Arbor Road
Croft
Nr Leicester
7/8/40

Elsie Dear
I know you will forgive me butting in on your ultra hectic time of feeding and entertaining a super family to say 'How do'.
I hope this finds you in your usual abundance of vitality and good spirits and that you have miraculously found some precious minutes for relaxation and recreation to maintain the balance.
You are highly honoured! as being the first person to whom I have written since my return to Croft so happily with you last Weds. I am pleased to report everything in the pink and I am by now almost accustomed to the new conditions and surroundings. Naturally I found the air and rooms rather oppressive, but now I do not feel so sensitive about it.
On Thursday I took a long walk around Croft. Friday went to Leicester with Mrs B. Sat. went to the farm at Cosby Hill 'per cycle', Sunday another walk around Croft, Monday cycle ride to Frolesworth, Leire, and Broughton Astley. Tuesday went to farm at Cosby Hill again and as the ground is high at this point the air is more akin to that of Markfield, so I appreciate the opportunity of being there.
You will see, therefore, that I have been living a rural life almost. Have taken my rest hours very religiously and avoided getting over tired or fatigued.
Am looking forward to seeing you on Monday and should arrive sometime after midday. And I trust you will be able to find me something to do to keep me out of mischief.
So Elsie my dear, until then cheeribye, happy thoughts 'keep smiling thru'
To the gang 'happy landings'
With my love as always, affectionately

Cyril

To Mrs E.M. Hartell
"Uranus"
The Bradgate Guest House
Newtown Linford
Nr Leicester

3 Arbor Road
Croft
Nr Leicester
29/8/40

Elsie Dear
Just a line to say 'How do' and to say I arrived at Croft alright.
Thank you so very much for your very kind birthday greetings and your good advice re – rosy tinted specs, you should know from experience of the comments if some people are noted. I forgot to tell you I celebrated (all on my own cos no one else was available at the time) by going to see 'Top Hat' with Fred Astaire and Ginger Rogers. A bit frivolous you will say, but it was dancing and light music which suited my mood just then. It was my first cinema visit for nearly a year.
A big thank you, also, for looking after me so well last Monday. It was nearly like old times especially to have a peep at the 'high lights' of the forest again.
What has been the outcome of the farm property? Personally, I think the price ought to be lower under the circumstances that the place requires development before it can earn money. Undoubtedly your idea is a good one, given the necessary capital of the land sold at a more reasonable price in accordance with its face value.
I am taking my car out for debt, although I agree with you it is not worth the expense incurred for the mileage available, but I think it will do the car good after standing so long and a possible standing through another winter.
When I arrived at Leicester on Monday night I bumped into Howard and he has invited me to his bungalow on Sunday week. As this is the day before I visit the san again would it be possible for me to stay with you on the Sunday night? So that the one journey to Bradgate would answer for the Monday visit to the san as well.

I hope you haven't had any disturbed nights with air raids. I have managed to sleep through, although have had two warnings since Sunday.
So Cheeribye dear, and sincere good wishes, Elsie, for the welfare of you and yours. My love to you.
Affectionately yours in all that is good, true, and beautiful

Cyril

To Mrs E.M. Hartell
"Uranus"
The Bradgate Guest House
Newtown Linford
Nr Leicester

19 Fellowes Rd
Old Fletton
Peterborough
10/10/40
Thurs

Elsie dearest

I do hope this letter finds you free from the pains and irritations that were hovering about when I left 'Uranus' and you, and that the new guests are jolly and charming as some compensation for the officious Woods.
Strange as it may seem from the pen of a cold Virgo, my thoughts have been so much with you even after two days away and I am longing to be close to you again. For this I put all the blame on you for being you.
I am pleased to report safe arrival at Peterborough (after a pleasant journey) at 7.30pm last night, and as 'a welcome home', the sirens sounded the warning as soon as I stepped into the house, however there was no activity and I was able to get a good night of rest and peace.

A pleasant surprise awaited me; my brother had arrived a few hours before me, having taken 'French leave' during his 24 hr rest period. This morning Elna and I saw him off on the 8.50 a.m. for Kings Cross. Since he has been in the London district he has been much in action with the guns and not getting much regular sleep and, therefore, he registered strain and tiredness, instead of looking really fit as on his last visit home. I was glad to note that army life has broadened his outlook, given him more self-reliance and self-discipline. His opinion of the war and politics in general is that it is a farce, and he jokes about all the 'red tape' and blunders and the illogical way of doing things in the army. Such is the criticism of youth upon the ways of its elders.

When I arrived at Croft on Tues, I found a communication from U.O. headquarters awaiting me. It included a "Shrine of Wisdom', also a form to fill up regarding a certain Elsie May and her progress for the past year etc. in the Orders System (3d). *I can conscientiously report good progress in spite of the difficulty of actual study. I do look forward to the time when we can resume a study of the lectures, although the outlook is not too rosy at present.*

I hope you have not been called out for F.A.P. (21) *duty until you get a reserve of sleep!!? but I expect by the time I see you again you will have rendered your other piece of national service in aiding the swelling of the birth rate but not in AJF2* (22) *I hope.*

My brother sends his greetings and good wishes, also mother and Elna. The latter are looking much better and don't worry so much now over air raids. I am taking them to see a George Formby film tomorrow (Friday). Today I am visiting Harold's father. By the way, Harold's year of birth was 1904, May 8th. Will try to get time for you.

Well darling, I will now close down after telling you that I am returning to Croft on Monday night and will come out to Uranus on Tuesday arriving about 6 to 7pm.

Yours, my dear, in all that is Good, True, Beautiful. As always, my deepest affection and love

Cyril

To Mrs E.M. Hartell
"Uranus"
The Bradgate Guest House
Newtown Linford
Nr Leicester

19 Fellowes Rd
Old Fletton
Peterborough
12/10/40

Elsie darling

I was so happy to receive your letter this morning (Sat). It was very sweet of you to spare me some of your valuable time to contact me via pen and paper.

I am so glad to hear that the spot of bother and nuisance value of Mr Woods has been overcome and he is treating you with the respect you always deserve, dearest.

So glad to learn also, that the piece of National Service has been concluded successfully with no accidents.

Was most interested and amused over your mention of a further influx of H.M. couples (23) *, its sure getting a speciality, and my suggestion that this branch of service be written on the advert board and bill heads is not apparently out of place. I note that Mrs. Adams has interesting information to report upon the subject when I return. However, I am always willing to listen to anything of educational value in all branches!!*

We are still having raid warnings every night but so far there has been no activity to cause me to lose my sleep and, like you, I am having lots of sleep, and putting some by for reserve (like the squirrel).

Nothing eventful has happened to me except that in going out with Elna, I am getting her a bad character for flirting as people think it is another boy.

Well darling, I shall soon be with you again. A week is too long to be away I realise, and my thoughts gravitate to you at every opportunity.

May all good be with you and yours until we meet. My mother and Elna send their love.

Keep smiling thro', Elsie dearest, and you know that my deepest affection and love for you is sure, sweetheart.

As always

Cyril

Chapter 14
The Second World War Ends, Healing, The Farm, Pete, Pam and Tony, Joan Stretton

Elsie's children spent several years growing up in Newtown Linford which would have given them a great sense of fun and freedom with Bradgate Park just across the road. Alma their cousin recalls sleeping with her sister and cousins on camp beds in the garage. She remembers clearly Peter's sense of mischief in making 'apple pie beds' and tying their nightclothes together when they weren't looking.

Peter started work as a farm hand on Burrows Farm, Cropston, in 1942 aged 14. Mr Burrows, referred to in the last letter from Cyril, was a farmer who Pam and Peter worked for and would often refer to Peter as 'Clandyke' or 'Alf'. As a farmer Peter had a 'reserved occupation' and wasn't accepted into the forces. Tony remembers that Peter also took a post as Assistant Warden at Bradgate Park between the age of about 15 and 17 under the supervision of a Mr. Middleton, until he was old enough to join the Army. He had volunteered for the Army and 'couldn't get in quick enough' due to village gossip and aspersions that he had avoided being called up, which was untrue. He joined up aged 19 on 26th September 1947 with the Royal Army Service Corps working with horses and as a driver. Peter served in Aldershot and the MELF Canal Zone in Egypt and achieved Lance Corporal. On discharge in February 1953 his conduct and character on discharge were described as 'exemplary', 'of quiet disposition, honest, sober and trustworthy, always cheerful and popular with his colleagues'. Tony began his National service aged 18 in 1948 serving in Hamburg, and in The British Army of The Rhine, Hanover, Germany, achieving the rank of Lance Corporal. He worked as a clerk itemizing and checking the personal effects of soldiers who had died overseas having to remove sensitive or illegally held items such as blood stained clothing or guns before they could be packaged into hessian parcels and sent on to the families of the deceased. During short periods of leave, Tony and a fellow soldier visited a ski resort in the Harz Mountains, the Monhe Dam (featured in the Dam Busters film) and the Fresian Islands as well as a 3-day visit to a Russian occupied sector of Berlin where they had their first sighting of Russian soldiers. This time saw Tony grow from an 18 year old boy to a man ready to take his place in the adult world.

Pamela left school at 16 and helped Elsie to run the guesthouse before joining the Women's Land Army as her contribution to the war effort.

In these letters dated August 1945 Elsie had gone to stay at Healing in Grimsby the home of Cyril's relatives and was recovering from an illness or an operation. Cyril, Pam, Peter and Tony were holding the fort at the guesthouse and helping out at Burrows Farm.

When Peter returned from Egypt in 1953, after Elsie had bought him out of the Army, she had sold the Guesthouse and bought a farm at Thornton in Leicestershire with Cyril.

To Mrs E.M. Pamphilon
C/o Mrs R. Smith
Sunny Dene
Poplar Rd
Healing
Nr Gt Frimsby
Lincs

Newtown Linford
Aug 23rd 1945

My darling
Many, many thanks for your letter received this morning with all its good wishes for my birthday etc.
I am so glad to learn that you are not feeling so tired as during your last stay at Healing. I guess that within a few days you will be able to take full benefit of your holiday.
Everything is going on smoothly at home and Tony is managing very well indeed for a mere male. The meals have been ready for us when required. Wednesday evening and tonight also, the farming experts have been working late and Tony has left after his 6 pm meal with me to go to the farm to give a hand. It is now 9 pm and I expect them home very soon. Tinker is at my feet as I write, after ordering me to put the ducks to bed, and now he waits for his milk and biscuits.
Today the weather has been showery and cool.
Yesterday I went to Stony Stratford (not far from Dunstable) to a laundry where we have to lay a concrete foundation for a steam boiler. I went with the engineers supplying the boiler etc. They took me in their car. I enjoyed the journey; it was a change from travelling by train, the two days previous.
It does seem strange not to see my Elsie May when I arrive home in the evenings; that is when I miss you most of all. I certainly don't want to revert back to 'bachelorhood' after three days of free lance.
I too hope that next year we can celebrate my birthday together and maybe also a fortnight's holiday together.
We have not had a call from the doctor yet so presume he trusts that you were able to get away inspite of the difficulties which were apparent at the time he last saw you.

Pam is having her day off tomorrow (Friday).

Well my darling, I will send you a good night kiss before turning in. Keep smiling and I hope the weather will enable you to get many days near the sea side. My constant thoughts for your welfare and renewed strength. I look forward to seeing you soon (wishing it could be sooner)

My love sweetheart
Always yours

Cyril

PS. Kind thoughts to Aunt and Evelyn

PS. Did you go to Grimsby to see "Blythe Spirit"? I hoped you enjoyed the trips out. I hope also that the sorrows of the evil one are finding material for your brain and imagination to work upon. It is a book I should like to read again!! I believe at the end Satan is seen coming out of the Houses of Parliament if my memory serves me correctly. At the time I read it I found it very amusing in parts.

To Mrs E.M. Pamphilon
C/o Mrs R. Smith
Sunny Dene
Poplar Rd
Healing
Nr Gt Frimsby, Lincs

Newtown Linford
Thursday 26.8.45

My dearest

Your letter arrived safely on Saturday morning together with Tony's shoes (which by the way are a good fit).

I hope the weather is as nice at Healing as it is just now at Bradgate. It is 2 pm; Pam is just off to the farm. I am sitting in the 'downstairs front' writing and I can hear the noise of people in the park and the vehicles bringing them out. Pete has the Sunday off and he and Tony have just gone out for a walk.

With regard to their holiday it seems that it will be O.K. if you are able to find them a berth. By the way, they expect to finish the harvest by Monday or Tuesday and on Friday evening Mr Burrows is having the usual harvest supper so I don't know whether Pete would feel like travelling after the 'Beano'. However I shall come down on the Sat and we should return on the Sunday. Pam would have the Sat off to help get the boys off if they get fixed up.

This weekend we had Joan (24) *over. Came Sat. evening and will return 5.30 this evening. She and Pam did cleaning and cooking today, so we found her helpful.*

I thought of you and I on Friday celebrating behind a glass of gin and lime but it turned out to be only wishful thinking. You say you are missing me very much, I bet you are not missing me half as much as I am you. My sole consolation is the fact that it is for the benefit of your health, so must not be impatient. When you come back better in health and rested that will be the best reward for a lonely husband like yours truly.

Pam went to get her Land Army clothes during her day off on Fri. She bought a pair of socks for my birthday. Elna sent me a card. Enclosed some letters from Colin, which I am sending to you. I enclose also a cutting from the 'Mirror' which I think faithfully depicts the clothes outlook for the next few months. 'Never mind, eh'.

I hope you received my last letters which I sent you on Wednesday and Friday morning respectively.

Well how is the fish trade? Have associated tasty fish meals with you when my mind frequently wanders into thoughts of you and what you may be doing. I expect by now you will have acquired that atmosphere of 'retiredness' typical of Healingites. Slow, easy and comfortable really; just what you want. Expect also you will return with a trace of dialect savouring of the north. I am sorry to learn that you still have the pain. I do so hope that by now it has disappeared and that the next week will prove to be a painless one and with a feeling of returning strength.

You mention Pam and Pete, getting wet. No, last week they managed to keep dry inspite of odd showers.

Tonight I shall go to church and let Mr Bland know about time off next Sunday for someone to take my turn. I shall think of you whilst I am there and missing you from by my side.

What do you think of the Siddens lifting of lease and lend? I trust that some other system will take its place with similar benefits to tide us over the next 12 months.

Well I am closing so that Joan can post this letter before 4.20.

Keep smiling through my darling – heaps of affectionate thoughts and a parting kiss with all my love.

From your sweetheart

Cyril

Family and friends 1940's onwards

Left: Marion and George Richardson. Marion was a good friend of Elsie's and supported her through her early days of widowhood. She was also Tony's Godmother

Right: Elsie

Above: Cyril

Back left: Elsie, Cyril, Pamela, Front left: Peter and Tony.

From left: Elsie, Tony and Cyril at the back of the Guesthouse

Elsie and Peter

Peter and Tony

Elsie and Tinker at the back of the guesthouse

Cyril and Elsie in the 1940's

Above: Walter and Ethel Stretton (nee Martin)

Above: Peter (left) and Tony in 1949. Below: Tony (left) and Peter in 2006. One of Elsie's paintings in the background

Above: Women's Institute, Thornton, Leicestershire, Elsie is third from the right on the front row.

Elsie left: with grandchildren John and Sally in the early 1960's and right in a 1975 newspaper article describing Elsie as 'loved by all' and 'the salt of the earth'

Chapter 15
Memories of Thornton

Elsie and Cyril bought a farmhouse at Thornton, Leicestershire contained in about 6 acres of land overlooking the reservoir. They established a dairy farm known as Reservoir Farm. Peter and Pamela managed the farm, and a valuable asset of 30 acres of land in another part of the village for which they had taken over the rental. Peter married one of his milk customers, Carol Bogan, and they made their first home in a caravan at the back of the cowshed before moving to Old Hall Farm, Bardon. Eventually Reservoir Farm was sold, and one of the plots which had been the orchard was retained. It was on this site that Elsie and Cyril built 'Red Brick Bungalow' the home remembered fondly by Elsie's grandchildren and great grandchildren.

Cyril (Grandpa Pamphilon) often referred to Elsie as Mrs P. while the members of the Women's Institute in the village knew her affectionately as Mrs Pam.

Elsie was a strong activist writing a number of letters and articles in support of various causes such as campaigning for a bus for schoolchildren, and her drinking water 'anti-fluoride' campaign. In her article for 'The Socialist Leader' in 1948 she described life before WW1 including the 'Tally man', the 'Pawnbroker' the 'utter hopelessness' of poor living conditions, lack of work, and debt incurred by families at the beginning of the century. Her experiences and the people she met throughout her life no doubt formed her determined nature and fuelled her resolve to make a difference where she could. In 1971 she wrote a moving story in the Leicester Mercury about the plight of Gipsies particularly Rose Boswell, a Gipsy princess who died from 'galloping consumption' (tuberculosis) and was buried in St Mary's Church, South Luffenham, Leicester.

Elsie became president of the 'Thornton Women's Institute' (WI) from 1955 to 1967/68, was vice president for a year. From 1973 to 1985 she was an active committee member and 'Press Correspondent'. An interview for the Leicester Advertiser in 1975 described her as 'one of those the salt of the earth people' and 'loved by all' a play on the meaning of her Greek surname. It also said that her first love was painting followed by writing. Muriel Walker who is now the President at Thornton WI recalls that Mrs Pam was dearly loved and she became very much part of the village community. She played a great part in organising a 'Lady Jane Grey' pageant and it is believed that she wrote some of the scenes.

Mrs Pam was a fount of information and spent some happy times with Muriel. They shared a love of literature and history, swapping books and talking about children's welfare, as Muriel was a teacher and a young mother at the time. Alma, Elsie's niece remembers her Aunt Elsie's love of books and recalls her taking a book on her walks around Thornton Reservoir, and stopping half way to read before walking around the rest of the circumference of the beauty spot. Elsie never lost her love of books. During the 1990's Elsie and Marianne, her grandson Nigel's then girlfriend, would have regular Saturday fish and chip lunches at the bungalow. They would talk about books and Marianne was given one of the 'Lady Jane Grey' booklets that Elsie wrote which is now a treasured possession.

Elsie often helped out at the Thornton baby clinic down the years. Her granddaughter Linda recalls on the birth of her own daughter Emma in the early 1980's, receiving a 'talking to' from Grandma about the benefits of one brand of baby milk over another which Grandma deemed to be 'rubbish'! Elsie had very strong opinions.

Nigel also remembers his Gran's indignation at being stopped by the police for speeding at 35 mph in a 30 mph zone in Bagworth. In her 80's Elsie became a little heavy on the clutch in her car. Her son Peter and his son in law Robert needed to change the clutch three times within a very short time period. Elsie never admitted to driving with her foot on the clutch as well as the accelerator but the evidence was conclusive!

Although the bungalow at Thornton had under floor heating, a large gloss painted heating pipe, fascinating to children, and about the thickness of a drainpipe, ran along the living room windowsill overlooking the reservoir. Most of Elsie's grandchildren and some great grandchildren over the years will have run little fingers over and under the tactile pipe to feel its comforting warmth and secretly peel off little particles of chipped paint. In her latter years Elsie often recalled to Linda a memory of a little boy called Jason who she had told not to touch the pipe because it was hot - and he touched it anyway! It had slipped her memory that Jason was her great grandson, Linda's son!

Nigel has fond memories as a child of having to polish the brasses, especially the trumpet, which all the grandchildren would have endeavoured to get a sound out of during visits, mostly without success. He also remembers when he was older having to take down the secondary glazing from the very large living room window with the reservoir view. After Elsie had finished cleaning it he remembers being told 'don't touch the glass', probably quite difficult when having to replace the window.

The bungalow had from a child's perspective the 'biggest bathroom in the world' with the very distinctive smell of Pears soap which wafted over when the bathroom door was opened. Crockery in the kitchen, including a large milk jug, was always blue and white striped. A little silver sugar bowl held the solid, white frosted lumps which were a novelty at every visit. A pair of silver sugar tongues, with practice, as dexterity improved, precariously manoeuvred the little sweet squares from the bowl into children's mouths!

As young children it was always incredibly amusing and mysterious when Grandma with a twinkle in her eye, retrieved her handkerchief, always kept 'up her knicker leg', from her 'bloomers' which almost reached her knees! Elsie May was a woman of small stature but many talents!

Cyril died unexpectedly in September 1971 leaving Elsie once again a widow. He is buried in Thornton Churchyard. Elsie lived at the bungalow that she and Cyril had built until she died on July 16th 1997 aged 98. Her final goodbye was at Newtown Linford Anglican Church and she is buried at the cemetery on the road between Newtown Linford and Groby.

Above: Elsie and below: three children of three sisters.
From left: Alma Ethel's Daughter, middle, Peter Elsie's son, and right Shirley, Emma's daughter

Epilogue to the Life of Elsie May Pamphilon by Jackie Harris (nee Hartell) Elsie and Harold's granddaughter, via Tony Hartell

This fascinating collection of personal letters, recently uncovered in my late uncle's bureau, has offered a great insight into the life of a woman I did not know, barely met, but felt some affinity for.

Elsie May was my paternal grandmother. Due to a family rift when I was a young child, I had not had any contact with her until I asked my father if I could go with him to visit her when I was about 14 years old.

I was fascinated to know more about her. I remember my dad giving me a little talk on the way, saying it didn't matter how old he was, she would still remind him to wipe his feet when we got there.

I think I was expecting a very strict and scary lady, but I could see the twinkle in her eye and could feel a sense of love exuding from her, although she was not the sort of person to show it outwardly.

Like Sally, I too remember birthday and Christmas gifts from Grandma Pamphilon of beautiful hardback books of the classics – poetry and novels, which I would pour over on rainy days, with neat italic handwritten inscriptions in the front cover.

The greatest gift my grandmother has passed down through my father is his enormous love of Bradgate Park.
Some of the best sledging was to be had from the top of Old John.

Most weekends when I was a child would be spent walking and playing in one part or another of this wonderful public parkland, and my dad would tell me stories of his childhood escapades in and around the park – climbing over the fence when it was officially closed to run wild at boyhood games with his big brother, Peter; a brush with death when he fell off a high rocky outcrop (he still bears the scar on his forehead), pond-dipping for tiddlers in the stream and prized deer antlers found after the rutting season.

My dad must have learnt a lot from his hours in this natural landscape. He knew the best places to pick mushrooms and watch badgers at dawn, which he shared with me, and I will be eternally grateful for those experiences.

Reading through the letters I notice that I share my grandmother's love of sleeping outside. Any opportunity I got as a child I would build some sort of makeshift shelter in the garden and beg to sleep in it. I am also fascinated by religion and have spent much of my life avoiding the organised variety but investigating the different views of each in a bid to understand the fundamental truths they are each seeking.

I don't know how much of this is genetic or merely wishful thinking – grasping for some sort of link with my family heritage, but it doesn't really matter.

What I have come to conclude is that my grandmother was quite an extraordinary woman, especially for the time in which she lived.

Here we are in 2018 still discussing feminism and equality for women. Elsie May was a woman who just got on and did what she needed to do and believed was right, and achieved a great deal in her long and productive life.

Some of her talents are barely mentioned, but apparently she wrote stories, (one or more broadcast on the radio). She compiled and published a pamphlet on Lady Jane Grey, drove an ambulance during the war, was a member of numerous societies, a school governor, a founder of Thornton WI, and took astrology very seriously.

She was clearly strong, independent, and a force to be reckoned with. Her tenacity in the face of adversity can only be admired.

I am so glad these letters came to light, and am even more glad that my cousin Sally has had the patience, tenacity and sheer will to herd them into such legible order. This is a fascinating social history that I hope will appeal further afield than the immediate family and those who knew Elsie May.

Huge thanks to Barry and Jeanette McNeil - present owners of Uranus, the former guesthouse - who were kind enough to allow us into their home on 24.4.2016 (Tony's 86th birthday) to rekindle some of the memories of my father's childhood there.

It made my day when my father walked into the hall and immediately exclaimed that he had slid along the wooden floor with dusters on his feet to polish it many a time, and so the afternoon continued........

"Children in the Apple Tree"

"We shall not cease from exploration
And at the end of all our exploring
Will be to arrive where we started
And know the place for the first time.

Through the unknown, unremembered gate
When the last of earth left to discover
Is that which was the beginning;
At the source of the longest river
The voice of the hidden waterfall
And the children in the apple-tree

Not known because not looked for
But heard, half-heard, in the stillness
Between two waves of the sea.
Quick now, here, now, always-
A condition of complete simplicity
(Costing not less than everything)
And all shall be well and
All manner of thing shall be well
When the tongues of flames are in-folded
Into the crowned knot of fire
And the fire and the rose are one".

From 'The Four Quartets (Little Gidding)' by T.S Elliot.
(Licence to print granted by kind permission of Faber and Faber Ltd, publishers)

Elsie and Harold's eldest great grandchildren and youngest great great grandchildren to date in Peter's apple tree

Left to right:
Emma and Phoebe, Claire and Albert

Appendix A

1. Marion Richardson was Elsie's friend, as referred to in the prologue. She was also Tony's Godmother. Marion's cottage, the stone cottage near the main entrance to the gates of Bradgate Park was her home and she kept a little café across the road from the guesthouse. It is now the Visitor Centre and Tea Rooms and was named after her. It was officially opened by the Bradgate Park Trust Management Committee on 25th May 1976. Marion lived in the cottage before her death in 1974 and had done much for Newtown Linford residents, including starting the records which Janet Neaverson now holds *(The Newtown Linford Church Magazine 2012)*

2. Cameronians (Scottish Rifles). In 1915 the Cameronians were travelling the Leicestershire area recruiting. Quite often men were moved around to neighbouring regiments when numbers suffered and they transferred when their skills were in demand. The Rifle Corps recruited most of their number through other Regiments *(Information from Ian Vickers, Ibstock Historical Society).*

3. Probably a reference to a practice learned in the study of Theosophy - The Theosophical Society studied various religions, such as Buddhism and Hinduism and was an organization that Harold and Elsie were part of. They also practiced 'concentration' on each other to send positive 'vibrations' which becomes evident in later letters. It could be perceived to be a kind of prayer. The Theosophical Society was founded by Helena Petrovna Blavatsky, Henry Steel Olcott, William Quan Judge, in New York City on November 17, 1875. Today, students belong to any religion in the world, or to none, and are united by the society's objectives by their wish to remove religious antagonism and to draw together men of goodwill whatsoever their religious opinions, and by a desire to study religious truths and share the results of their studies with others. They hold that 'Truth' should be sought by study, reflection, purity of life, and devotion to high ideals. They regard 'Truth' as a prize to be striven for, not a dogma to be imposed by authority. They extend tolerance to all, even to the intolerant, and see every religion as an expression of the Divine Wisdom and prefer its study to its condemnation, and its practice to

proselytism. Peace is their watchword, and Truth is their aim. (http://www.theosophicalsociety.org.uk).

3a. 'American Theosophist' – a publication of the society, in which Miss Clara M. Codd wrote articles about the inner life.

3b. Ancient Wisdom – a reference to Theosophy

3c. The Theosophical Society held a Summer School and Cyril makes reference to a Summer Retreat

3d. Orders system – progression route in Theosophy

4. Harvey (name has been changed) – Seems to be a key member of the local Theosophy Society group and he co-ordinated some of the meetings for which Elsie opened up her home.

5. Schneider Trophy - The **Coupe d'Aviation Maritime Jacques Schneider**, commonly called the **Schneider Trophy** or **Schneider Prize** (sometimes incorrectly referred to as the Schneider Cup, a different prize), was a trophy awarded annually (and later, biannually) to the winner of a race for seaplanes and flying boats. The Schneider Trophy is now held at the Science Museum, South Kensington, London. Announced in 1912 by Jacques Schneider, a French financier, balloonist and aircraft enthusiast, the competition offered a prize of approximately £1,000. The race was held twelve times between 1913 and 1931. It was intended to encourage technical advances in civil aviation but became a contest for pure speed with laps over a (usually) triangular course (initially 280 km, later 350 km). The contests were staged as time trials, with aircraft setting off individually at pre-agreed times, usually 15 minutes apart. The contests were very popular and some attracted crowds of over 200,000 spectators. An earlier trophy, also presented by Jacques Schneider in 1910, in France, was the Schneider Cup, which is now in the possession of the RAF College, Cranwell (https://en.wikipedia.org/wiki/SchneiderTrophy)

In 1929 the Schneider Trophy Contest was again held in England, at Calshot, on September 7th. The start and finish of the 186 mile course was located at Cowes, and there were turning points at Sea View (Isle of Wight), a point about 6 miles South of Hayling Island and Southsea. Great Britain and Italy entered 3 teams of aircraft each. France was unable to enter a team and a United States entry by Al William's failed to participate. (http://www.hampshireairfields.co.uk/airfields/schneider1929.html)

6. Ken and Jan – family friends of Elsie and Harold. Ken, who was married to Jan and was a painter and decorator, who used to pop in and do jobs around the guesthouse. They lived in one of the bungalows on the way out of Newtown Linford. They decorated part of the guesthouse after blasting from Groby Quarry caused damage.

7. T. (Tom) Baggott was a rounds man with the Co-op Bakery

8. Carl Brisson was a Danish film actor and singer (24.12.1893-25.09.1958)

9. Walter Stretton - was married to Ethel Maud, Elsie's sister. They had two children, Joan and Alma. Walter worked as 'Dock Manager Foreman' for milkman's delivery rounds with the Co-op Dairy at Glenfield.

10. It is possible that George was the husband of Marion Richardson, referred to by Tony in the prologue. He was a Bradgate Park Estate Worker. There was also another George who was a carpenter and a bachelor who also used to pop into the guesthouse to do odd jobs. Tony admired him as a child and aspired to be either a Carpenter or a Bachelor when he grew up.

11. 'The San' - a reference to Markfield Sanatorium/Hospital, Leicestershire

The County Sanatorium and Isolation Hospital (the "Markfield Hospital") was opened in September 1932 by Sir George Newman, the Chief Medical Officer to the Ministry of Health.

There were 203 beds in six wards, with isolation for fever patients and a sanatorium for patients with tuberculosis (TB). As well as wards, there was a chapel, two mortuaries, a laundry, a swimming pool and tennis courts. Fever patients were separated from visitors by glass screens, so parents and children had to communicate as best they could. Letters were the main way of keeping in touch for most patients.

12. **Huts** at the sanatorium housed patients with TB and diphtheria, and were burnt after use and replaced by new ones. (*Cyril's letter of 18.04.1940 seems to contradict this).* http://www.markfieldhistory.btck.co.uk/MarkfieldHospital. *(The information above has been used with kind permission of the Markfield History Group. Information on the website is mainly from the booklet "Memories of Markfield Hospital" produced by the Markfield Local History Group in 2006).*
TB treatment in sanatoria up until 1944 was a combination of sunlight, diet, and gentle exercise. Treatment may not have improved survival rates but by removing people with the infection from the community disease transmission would have been reduced. Various types of surgery were introduced in the 1930's in an attempt to obliterate the lung cavities that developed including collapsing the lung, introducing air to the pleural cavity. PAS treatment (para-aminosalycilic acid combined with streptomycin) was introduced in the late 1940's. Streptomycin was given by intramuscular injection and was painful for patients and PAS was given in large quantities as a drink and caused nausea (Davies P. 1999).

13. Sam (name has been changed) used to come to the guesthouse to help out make himself useful around the place. He was a university student and was quite an effeminate young man. He and Elsie developed a friendship. Tony thinks that people thought he was Elsie's lover. This may be the 'Sam' referred to by Cyril.

14. Colin was Cyril's younger brother. He had a romantic liaison with Pam, Elsie and Harold's daughter. Colin was based at Devizes where there was an Army Depot and he was involved in Radio Communications.

15.'The gang' – Cyril's pet name for Pamela, Peter and Tony, Elsie's children.

16.Rupert Brooke (3 August 1887 – 23 April 1915) was an English poet known for his idealistic war sonnets written during the First World War, especially "The Soldier". He was also known for his boyish good looks, which were said to have prompted the Irish poet Yeats to describe him as "the handsomest young man in England" (https://enwikipedia.org/wiki/Rupert_Brooke)

17.Howard was a carpenter and family friend who lived in one of the bungalows situated on the way out of Newtown Linford in the opposite direction to Anstey

18.Circs – circumstances

19.Elna was Cyril's sister

20.A.R.P – 'Air Raid Precautions' were organised by the government and carried out by local authorities to protect civilians from danger in air raids. The Air Raid Wardens Service was created and manned by volunteers who patrolled the streets during blackouts to ensure that no light was visible. They also reported the extent of bomb damage to assess the need for emergency services, were responsible for handing out gas masks and organising air raid shelters. (www.primaryhomeworkhelp.co.uk/war/wardens)

21. F. A. P. Abbreviation 'For All Purposes' a term used in the Royal Airforce.

22. AJF2 - referred to in one of Cyril's letters was the registration number of the Ford 8 car.

23. H.M. - Honeymoon couples

24. Joan was Ethel and Walter Stretton's daughter, and cousin to Pam, Peter and Tony. She helped out in the guesthouse and had a younger sister called Alma.

Appendix B

Elsie's Family History

(Some of the detail in this section has been repeated from the main text, it has been left in to give a full picture. The information has been laid out as chronologically as possible).

Elsie's Parents and Grandparents

Emma Sarah Martin (nee Joyce/Dixon-Taylor), Elsie's mother, was born on July 20th 1879 in Oundle, Nothamptonshire. She moved to Leicester with her parents Dinah (nee Dixon) and William Joyce, a sailor, also from Northamptonshire.

> **About Dinah Dixon/Taylor** (1848-1910) Dinah was unable to read and write as she signed Emma Sarah's birth certificate in 1879 with a cross. Emma Sarah was born in, Oundle, Northampton. The 1901 census records that Dinah Taylor, 21 Hawthorne St, Leicester was a widow, she was living with Emma Sarah and Henry at 21 Hawthorne Street at the time of Elsie's birth. Dinah died aged 61 in July 1910 and was buried at Gilroes Cemetery,
>
> **About William Joyce** (1854-1898) William Joyce was a sailor who deserted from the navy took his family in a hurried move to Leicester where they had relatives. They unofficially changed their name to Taylor, subsequent children being registered Dixon-Taylor.

Henry Martin, Elsie's father, also known as Harry, in June 1875 in Notting Hill, Kensington, London. When he was 15 his parents Joel Martin and Mary Ann Martin (nee Vincent) moved to Silsoe, Bedfordshire where they managed the Lord Nelson public house and later The Blackbirds Inn, Flitwick, Bedfordshire.

About Joel Martin (1837-1901) Henry's father was a Licensed Victualler (publican) and had been a master carpenter and the village undertaker. There is a family story about his death that says he severed the palm of his thumb in a carpentry accident and bled to death while being taken to hospital on the back of a pony and trap. There is no concrete evidence to back up the story, and his death certificate says that he died in 1901 from hepatic cirrhosis and asthenia aged 62 years in Flitwick Road in the district of Ampthill. Joel is buried in Flitwick graveyard and his gravestone reads:

'Hush, blessed are the dead in Jesus arms who rest'

About Mary Ann Martin (1865-1909) Elsie's grandmother (also known as Margaret) would probably have been the children's main carer from 1905 to 1909; possibly with help her daughter May who lived with her. Joel her husband had died in Feb 1901. Mary Ann died on November 1909 from stomach cancer. Her obituary in the Luton Times and Advertiser on November 19th 1909, the day of her funeral, says that she and Joel ran the Blackbird Inn for nearly 18 years and that she was:

'of a quiet, unassuming and obliging disposition and was one of the most respected holders of licensed premises in Flitwick'. They were both natives and members of old Flitwick families, though they had spent some years away. Mrs Martin was one of a family of ten (Viincent), she leaves a family of four sons and two daughters'

On the same gravestone as Joel, Mary Ann's inscription reads:

'Blessed are the dead which die in the Lord for they rest from their labours'.

Emma Sarah and Henry's children

Emma Sarah and Henry Martin married on October 8th 1898 at Leicester Register Office. The marriage certificate said that she was 22 years although she was only 19, possibly because the age of consent in those days was 21.

Elsie May Martin was born on May 5th 1899 when Henry and Emma Sarah lived at 21 Hawthorne Street, off Beatrice Road in Newfoundpool. Emma Sarah and Henry had gone to live with Dinah and her three other children, Dinah (20), Eliza (16), and William (14) some time before Elsie was born.

Henry Martin, also known as Harry, was born in November 1900. In 1901 Henry and Emma Sarah moved to 11 Nook St, Newfoundpool, with Elsie and baby Henry. Henry died aged 14 at their Beatrice Road home from sunstroke/meningitis in the greenhouse.

Ethel Maud Martin was born on January 5th 1903.

Emma Martin, Henry and Emma Sarah's fourth child was born in July 1904. Emma Sarah died on July 30th 1904 aged almost 25 years of thrombosis and a pulmonary embolism, four days after giving birth to baby Emma. The family were living at 12 Ingle Street, Leicester at the time, Elsie was 5 years old when her mother died, Henry was 3 and a half, and Ethel was 18 months old.

After their mother's death in 1904, Elsie, Henry, and Ethel were sent to live at the home of Joel and Mary Ann Martin their paternal grandparents, The Blackbirds Inn, Flitwick in Bedfordshire. There is a question over whether Elsie and Ethel were brought up by separate relatives, as they seemed to be very different in outlook. Both sides of their own families however, were led to believe that they lived at least part of their early lives in Flitwick at the Blackbird Inn with their grandparent/s. Henry remarried in September 1905 to Evelyn Aldwinkle

Elsie's stepfamily

Sometime between November 1909 and 1911 after their grandmother Mary Ann's death, the children came back to Leicester to live. In 1911 when Elsie was 12, Harry 10 and Ethel 8 years they were living with Henry and Evelyn at 227 Beatrice Road, Leicester, along with Evelyn's son Sidney aged 6 years, and Evelyn and Henry's own two children James aged 2 years and baby Joel.

Evelyn Martin (nee Aldwinkle), Elsie's stepmother, was born in May 14th 1879. In 1900 aged 21 Evelyn worked as a servant to a Sarah Bass at 36 Ridley Street two doors away from her family who were living at 38 Ridley Street. In January 1905 Evelyn gave birth to a son in the Leicester workhouse after a local man she was engaged to let her down. Her parents disowned her and she was left on her own to have her baby who she named Sidney after her brother, the only person to support her after her son's birth. Family oral history says that Henry went to the workhouse to find someone to look after his four children after Emma Sarah died. Henry married Evelyn in Sept 1905 when she was 26. Evelyn died on November 26th 1955 at the Hillcrest Hospital, Leicester, the former workhouse.

Sidney Aldwinkle (1905-1988) was born to Evelyn on 11th January 1905 and was 8 months old when his mother married Henry. Evelyn is believed to have told Sidney that his father was a local boxer who got her and another woman pregnant although he had asked Evelyn to marry him. She was a proud woman, however, and refused the offer choosing instead to have her baby in the Leicester workhouse. Henry and Evelyn went on to have four more surviving children and Sidney always felt that Henry was unfair to him which led to a fight with his stepfather when he was 15 in which he knocked Henry out. Sid tried to run away to join the Army to avoid the conflict at home but was turned away as he looked too young. His mother agreed to write a letter, stating that he was older than he was, so that he could join up to get away from the difficult home situation.

After his Army career Sidney married twice and had one daughter, Mavis, from his first marriage to Dorothy Baker who was later known as Aunt Doris by Ethel's children Joan and Alma. Sid worked at the Imperial Typewriter Company on East Park Road in Leicester. At the start of the Second World War he volunteered for the Home Guard and while demonstrating how to use a gun, accidently shot himself in the stomach which almost killed him. He used the compensation he received to open an electrical shop on King Richards Road, Leicester. In the 1950's Sid's met his second wife Annie. During the 1940s and 1950s he was the General Manager of the Bars and Cafés at Butlin's holiday park in Skegness. He led his family to believe that he was a personal friend of Billy Butlin.

Henry and Evelyn's children

Although Henry and Evelyn had seven children of their own, three of them died in infancy. Their first two children to die were both buried in 1908, the same year that their third child Jim was born. The children were all brought up at 227 Beatrice Road, Newfoundpool, Leicester.

Charles Martin (1906-1908)

Arthur Martin (1907-1908) was born in December 1907 and died in February 1908.

James Harold Martin (1908-1986) Jim was born on Dec 25th 1908, he married Cynthia Hamilton and they lived in Canada. They had six children, Terry, Evelyn (Ev), Cynthia, Bob, Anita and Alan. They also had Madeliene, a war child, who was born while Jim was in the Army. Sadly, Madeliene died before he was demobbed and Jim never met his daughter.

Joel Martin (1910-1976) known as 'Joe' was born on June 18th 1910. He married Emma May Martin (no relation) on May 20th 1933 and they had seven children, James Henry 'Jim', Thomas Joel 'Joe', Hazel Mary, Eveline Annie, Rodney John, David, and Malcolm. He served in the Home Guard during the 1939-1945 war and in the Royal Engineers in India and Malaya until 1946. Joel achieved 'Acting Sergeant Major' in the Royal Engineers, and was an engineer at the Imperial Typewriter Company in Leicester most of his working life. He formed a debating society at Newfoundpool Working Men's club of which he was president and was known at the club as 'Honest Joe'. He was a verger of St. Augustine's Parish Church Newfoundpool and was known to have a private and quiet faith. Joel lived in Alma Street, Newfoundpool at the time of his father Henry's death in 1944.

Florence Eva Martin (1912-1980) known as 'Eva', married George Large in the summer of 1935 in Leicester. Although they wanted a family Eva was unable to conceive and they decided to adopt a child. During the adoption process Eva found she was pregnant. By the time her child Martin was born, she had adopted a little boy Paul, who was only a few months older than Martin. Paul sadly died as a young man. Eva and George lived at 16 Henley Crescent, Leicester and attended the Elim Pentecostal Church on Narborough Road. Eva was a devout Christian with a very strong faith and strong views. She died on June 1st 1980.

John William Martin (1914-1914)

George Henry Martin (1915-1995) known as Georgie, married Edna M. Cluley in 1937. They had three children, George (Georgie), Sandra, and Jeffrey.

Henry and Evelyn

Henry was a strict father and most definitely 'the head of the household'. Joel's son Jim remembers his father recalling how Henry's children had to sit in a row and wait for him to come in for his meal. They were not allowed to eat until he had finished his meal. Henry was strict even as a grandfather. When he worked on the construction of the Co-op in Leicester Forest East he would pop in to see Ethel and her children for tea and the children would have to remember their manners at the table. He is remembered fondly though, and was always interested in the children and their school work. Henry died on August 12th 1944 aged 69 at Hillcrest Hospital, the former workhouse, from 'cerebral degeneration, arterial sclerosis and myocarditis'.

Evelyn was very much loved by her grandchildren from her son Joel's marriage although Ethel's children remember her as a bit austere. Alma, Ethel's daughter has memories of going into the front room to look at Evelyn's gallstones which were kept in a jar on the mantel piece above the fireplace. Evelyn remained at their Beatrice Road home until her death on November 26th 1955 aged 76, after spending some time in the Hillcrest Hospital, probably the same workhouse where her life with Henry began.

Ethel and Emma as Adults

Ethel, Elsie's sister fell down the stairs when she was about 13 years old which affected her hearing and remained very deaf for the rest of her life. In 1923 she married Walter Stretton in Leicester and they lived at Leicester Forest East. Walter worked for the Co-op dairy on Glenfield Road, Leicester, as a milkman and then inside as a foreman. They had two children Joan, born in 1924, and Alma, born in 1931. Ethel had her first hearing aid for Alma's wedding so that she would be able to hear her daughter's wedding vows. Ethel was a very industrious woman and was an avid knitter. Her other passion, was making jam and marmalade, pickling onions and making beetroot wine. Her grandson Brian Tingay has happy memories of collecting elderberries and elderflowers with her for wine making, and Alma recalls hearing from the lounge, the sound of exploding corks popping off the wine bottles in the pantry. Ethel, like Elsie kept rabbits and poultry to help feed her family during war time. Joan is mentioned in Cyril's letters in the 1940's as helping out at Elsie's guesthouse with cooking and cleaning. Walter retired at 58 due to rheumatoid arthritis. He died aged 64, and Ethel died in 1979 aged 76 years.

Emma married Leslie Harvey Gray her childhood sweetheart on 11th April 1925, at Saint Augustine's Parish Church, Newfoundpool when she was 20. They lived at 172 Pool Road and had 7 children, Kenneth, Sylvia, Harry, John, Shirley, Doreen and Stephen. Leslie developed leukaemia and died in November 1948 leaving Emma to bring up their family. Harry and Sarah Hobbs were a great support to her and their home became a second home for Emma's children. After her children were grown Emma worked in the hosiery industry and on retirement became involved with a senior citizen's club taking full advantage of trips and outings. Her other priority was spending time with her family. Emma died on July 6th 1986 aged 82.

Appendix C

(Some of the detail in this section has been repeated from the main text, and has been left in to give a full picture. The information has been laid out at chronologically as possible).

Harold's Family

Edith (nee Owen) Harold's mother was born in October 1876 in the Clifton area of Bristol. Her Father came from Llanelly in Carmarthenshire in Wales. She moved to Leicester when she was 4 years old with her father **John Owen** (b.1851), a leather currier, and **Elizabeth Ann Owen** (nee Hall)(1855-1925) who was from Wellingborough, Northamptonshire.

George Hartell (1876-1918), Harold's father was born in Stafford, Staffordshire on November 28th 1876. George's father also **George Hartell** (1848-1916) and his mother **Elizabeth (nee Bishop)** (1848-1902) originated from Staffordshire but were shoe finishers in Leicester from 1881 to 1891. They moved to Avins Yard, Long Street, Atherstone, Warwickshire and continued to work as shoe finishers. Later in life George senior was known as a 'Boot and Shoe Maker and Journeyman', after becoming skilled in his craft. When his wife Elizabeth died in February 1902 aged 53 they were living at 4 Avins yard, and he signed the death certificate with an X suggesting that he was unable to write. He continued to live at Avins Yard after Elizabeth's death until he died 14 years later in 1916. George his son and Edith lived periodically both in Leicester and in Avins Yard, Atherstone.

Edith and George married on the 28th September 1895 at Leicester Register Office when they were both 19 years old. George worked as a shoe finisher, following his father's trade and Edith was a cigar maker. Henry James Owen, Edith's brother, and Jane Hartell, George's sister were witnesses at their wedding. After they married they lived at 14 Burgess Road in Leicester, the home of Edith's maternal grandparents **James Hall** (1836-1905) who was born in Headingly, Yorkshire and **Harriet Hall (nee Knight**) (1837-1919), born in Wilby, Wellingborough, Northamptonshire. They all worked in the shoe trade.

Edith and George's children

Harold, Edith's first child was born on November 20th 1895 and Burgess Road would have been his home. He lived with his maternal great-grandparents James and Harriet Hall in his early years and by the time he was aged 15 in 1911 and was living with his maternal grandparents John and Elizabeth Owen at Craven Street, Leicester and working as a clerk, probably at the Co-op bakery where he spent most of his working life, except for his time in the Army.

George was born on 26**th** November 1897 in Leicester. On May 16TH 1907 young George aged 9 was admitted to the Desford Industrial School, a reform institution. His grandmother Elizabeth, who had cared for him in Atherstone, had died on February 8th 1902 aged 53 from 'exhaustion' and 'apoplexy' most likely a sudden death from a stroke. George was 5 years old when his grandmother died and it is likely that he was sent home to Leicester to live with his parents. George's sentence at the school was 'detention until 16' for being 'beyond control, truancy, dishonesty, and obtaining money under false pretences'. He was of slight stature 4 feet 0.5 inches, of fair complexion, blue eyes, and light brown hair. His nose is described as broad and long and he had small scars on the right side of his head. In 1911 aged 13 years, George was an 'inmate' at the school or farm with approximately 93 other boys. The address on the census at that time was The Heath, Bagworth, in the parish of Thornton and his occupation was 'tailor and school part time'.

The Desford School established in 1881, was considered revolutionary in its day offering education and a trade rather than punishment for truants and juvenile offenders. Boys were often admitted for what today would be seen as trivial offences such as 'loitering on the street'. The school was the only one of its kind in Leicestershire and boys came from all over the country. The name was changed to The Desford Boys School, in 1921. The village and parish boundaries appear to have changed slightly over the years and the building, now partially derelict, stands in the grounds of Kirby Grange, a residential area at Botcheston, Leicestershire.

On leaving the school in 1912, aged 15 years and 8 months George enlisted with the 1st Leicestershire Regiment initially in the Training Reserve deployed from Fermoy in the South of Ireland as he was too young to go into action. He was just over 5 feet tall and weighed 7 stones according to his Army medical. His school reference to the Army stated that he was of good moral character and suitable for enlistment as a Band Boy probably because he had played the cornet for four years in the school band. George enrolled as a musician and wrote to the Desford School saying that he liked the Army very much and keeping them informed of his whereabouts. He was transferred to India in January 1914 serving with the 2nd Leicestershire Regiment. On furlough in June 1915 he stayed at 57 Merridale Road in Leicester, with or near his family. In August 1915 he landed at Le Harve, France with The Duke of Wellington's West Riding Regiment, Battalion 10, and went on to fight in the 1st and 2nd battles of Passchendaele. George was killed in action in Flanders, France on 20**th** September 1917 aged 19 five years after joining the Army. It is likely that he died on the first day of the 'Battle of the Menin Road Ridge' which was the 'Third Battle of Ypres' fought between 20**th** Sept and 25**th** Sept 1917 (Liddle 2013). George's name is on the Tyne Cot Memorial, Zonnebeke, Belgium.

A memorial in the form of an avenue of trees was planted on the playing field at The Desford Boys School site. The names of the 56 'old boys' including George who were killed in the Great War are engraved on a piece of grey Swithland slate and can be seen at the far end of the avenue of horse chestnut trees. A memorial service has been held each year on Remembrance Sunday since 2014 on the site of the former school, arranged by Desford Parish Church and the Old Boys Network. George's name is also in the Golden Roll of Honour book at Leicester Cathedral for the men of Leicester and Leicestershire who died in the Great War. He was awarded The British War Medal and the Victory Medal. The 'Military History Sheet' which recorded his death in 1917, stated in the 'next of kin' section that his father's address was Avins Yard, Atherstone, but his mother

Edith's address on the same document was recorded as Leicester, indicating that the couple were living apart. However, it could be that Edith had moved back to Leicester during her husband's time in the Army making the addresses on the paperwork appear to be incorrect. Harold was also recorded on the form as 'brother living with grandmother' and was still residing at 1 Court A, Craven Street, Leicester.

Edith was born on March 21st 1899. She lived with her parents unlike Harold and George who were brought up by grandparents. Edith was a cigar maker in her younger days and used a small machine at home, a skill undoubtedly passed down from her mother.

Horace was born in May 1900, and died aged 11 months on June 23rd 1901 when the family were living at Leadenhall Street Cottages, Leicester. He died from pertussis (whooping cough), pneumonia and convulsions.

Florence Elizabeth, who was born in 1902, died aged 3 years on December 16th 1905 from pertussis (whooping cough), broncho pneumonia and convulsions. In 1902 the family had moved to Dyers Yard, Belgrave Gate, Leicester and George was employed as a Cotton Dyer's Labourer.

Frederick Thomas, born in July 1905, died only 5 weeks after Florence in January 1906 at 7 months old, also from whooping cough. Chicken pox, broncho pneumonia and convulsions were also cited as the cause of his death.

Evelyn Mary, born in June 1906 was one of the four children who survived to adulthood. Evelyn was seven years younger than Edith and nine years older than Walter, the youngest child to survive.

Hilda May was born in December 1907, seven months after George was sent to Desford Industrial School. Baby Hilda was only 4 months old when she died from broncho pneumonia and convulsions on January 1st 1908. Her mother's was still resident in Leicester.

John Henry born in 1909, contracted measles and pneumonia at 21 months and died on March 25th 1911. By this time the family had moved to Atherstone, near to George's father.

Atherstone

George and Edith, their children Edith 12, Evelyn 5, and George and Edith's niece Doris Stokes aged 11 were resident at 4 Avins Yard in 1911. Doris's sister Elizabeth Stokes aged 8 was living a few doors away at 14 Avins Yard with her grandfather and her uncle, Thomas Hartell, who was George's brother. Doris and Elizabeth's mother Jane, George's sister, had died 2 years earlier on January 12th 1909 in Leicester. She was 35 and the cause of death was pulmonary phthisis linked to TB. Jane was already a widow, and Edith who had been living in Leicester and was present at her death. George and Edith appear to have taken Jane's two girls to live with them at Atherstone. The family would have been resident at Avins Yard, Atherstone when Dr Herring's report was written in 1911 about the poor living conditions.

Walter Ernest was born to Edith in Sept 1915 in Leicester when Harold would have been 20. Their father had joined the Army in 1914 and Edith had moved back to Leicester. Walter was 3 years old when his father died in 1918 and was brought up by 'Eadie', most likely an affectionate name for either his mother or his sister. His sister Edith would have been 16 when he was born in Merridale Road, Leicester and she would undoubtedly have played a large part in his upbringing, especially as their mother Edith had at least one admission to the Towers Hospital in Leicester in 1923 when he was 8 years old.

Frank A. was born in April 1917. On Frank's birth certificate his mother's occupation is still 'a cigar maker'. Frank died in August 1917 aged 3 months old from gastro enteritis at 63 Merridale Road, Leicester. He was buried at Welford Road Cemetery, Leicester.

Doris A. was born in June 1918. Doris died aged 18 days old on 27th June 1918 from 'marasmus' which can be linked with influenza, premature birth, and malnutrition (Reid 2005). In 1918 and 1919 the world was in the grip of the Spanish influenza pandemic. Doris was buried on July 5th at Welford Road Cemetery, Leicester. Edith's home address was 48 Merridale Road, Leicester at the time, and the certificate stated that she was a 'former cigar maker'.

On September 8th 1914, George, Harold's father, had enlisted in The Royal Warwickshire Regiment. He served with the 10th 1st and 11th Battalions and was discharged from the Army on 12th December 1917, after receiving a penetrating gunshot wound to the head. He was brought back to Leicester and died on December 22nd 1918 aged 42, from a cerebral abscess caused by his injuries. Harold's sister Edith then aged 19 years was present at their father's death in the 5th Northern Hospital in Leicester a year after his discharge from the Army. The hospital was a 'Military Territorial Force Medical Unit' which later became the Fielding Johnson Building at the Leicester University Campus (www2.le.ac.uk). George was buried on December 28th 1918 at Welford Road Cemetery. His name can be seen on the WW1 memorial also at Welford Road Cemetery, on screen wall, 01.199. He was awarded the British War Medal and the Victory Medal.

A Mining Accident

Thomas Hartell was George's brother (Edith's brother in law) and lived with George their father at Atherstone.

Sometime before the First World War broke out in 1914 when George and Edith lived in Atherstone George took work as a miner, a 'hewer below ground' probably in the Atherstone area. In 1911 he was a shunter at the colliery railway. It may have been the Baddesley Colliery where his brother Thomas had also worked. Thomas was 9 years younger than George and was a 'Screenman' responsible for regulating the flow of water into a coal washer. He was required to stand on a staging 5 feet above ground. The report from the Baddesley Colliery Trustees said: *"The staging and fencing recently erected were incomplete".* On 31st January 1913, Thomas, according to the Trustees, *"thoughtlessly stepped backwards and one leg fell through an opening and he fell backwards on to one of the angle iron guards of a slack elevator which ruptured his right kidney."* He died in hospital in Birmingham the following day. The Trustees state *"The accident emphasizes the danger of starting such machinery before all staging and fencing has been completed"* (Web: uk coalmining accidents and deaths index).

The Atherstone Ball Game

For 800 years Atherstone has staged 'The Ball Game' which would have been witnessed if not played by George and his family while they were residents in the town. It is reputed to have started in the time of King John when boys from Leicestershire played a grudge match of football up and down Long Street against boys from Warwickshire for a bag of gold. Locals are still passionate about the game, now played for the ball itself, which is traditionally thrown out of an upstairs window to start the game. The last person in possession of the ball when time is called is the winner. The ball is greatly prized and the game is played every Shrove Tuesday between 3.00 and 5.00 pm attracting crowds of spectators.

Edith, Evelyn and Walter as adults

Edith

In 1920 Edith married William Brant and lived initially in rooms at Argyle Street, Leicester, and then moving to 45 Merridale Road, across the road from where her mother lived at number 48. William and Edith had six children, Edgar Howard, George William, Irene M. (died aged 14 months old), Derek, Gladys Margaret, and Lilian May. In 1939 they were still living at 45 Merridale Road, Leicester.

Edith had a hard life and always put others before herself. In later life she developed Parkinson's disease which affected her mobility making her shuffle. She belonged to the Methodist church and was often found to be helping her friends and neighbours. Edith fell and broke her hip while doing one of these errands. Her daughter Margaret who was expecting her youngest child at the time took Edith to hospital. A couple of days later some of the family came to see Margaret to tell her that Edith had died. Margaret intuitively knew that her mother had passed away and was able to tell them the exact time – her baby had turned in her womb at the moment that Edith died on February 9th 1963 aged 63 years. To sum her up in the words of her family "Edith had a heart of gold".

Evelyn

In 1925 Evelyn married Louis Mackness in Leicester and they had eleven children, Dennis, Louis Ernest, Barbara, Constance Rose (Connie), June Patricia, Anthony (Tony), Irene Margaret, Alan Graham, Kathleen (Kath), Mavis and Peter. Her first child was born in 1925 and the youngest in 1950. In 1939 the family lived in Astley Road, Leicester. Evelyn died in October 1994 aged 88 years.

Walter

In December 1934 Walter married Alice E. Orchard who had lived in Syston, Leicestershire all her life which is where they made their home. Alice worked as a shoemaker. Walter worked as a builder's labourer and then spent the 2nd World War in the Royal Artillery on coastal defense, stationed at Gorleston on Sea, St Margaret's Bay, and in the latter part of the war at Barkby a mile from his home. After the war ended he was a lorry driver for 25 for years for the old 'British Road Services', and then worked in a small factory two doors from where the family lived. They had three children; Barry, Peter, and David who drowned age 7 years in 1955 in the River Wreake by Syston Mill. Walter was a fairly quiet man and liked to go to the local Working Men's Club. He died aged 71 years in October 1986.

Edith, Evelyn and Walter remained close in their adult lives. Edith would take her children, Margaret and Lilian, to visit Evelyn when she lived just off Imperial Road in Leicester, and Margaret has memories of Walter and Alice visiting Edith on Sundays. Margaret attended the funeral of Walter's son David in Syston when she was 15. She went on her mother's behalf as Edith was unable to be there because of her poor health. Margaret had been unaware that her mother had an older brother Harold and Harold's family had been unaware of his siblings

Appendix D

Lady Jane Grey

Lady Jane Grey

of Bradgate Park

LADY JANE GREY

by E. M. PAMPHILON

ONE SHILLING

FOREWORD.

This booklet has been written in the hope that it will add interest to your visit to Bradgate Park. I would like to take this opportunity of thanking Mr. E. Haslegrave (who has been agent to the Bradgate Park Estate for thirty years) for the information I was able to derive from the pictures and documents which he so kindly lent to me; and to Mr. G. O. Walker, of Leicester Road, Blaby, to whom I am indebted for the photographs.

E. M. PAMPHILON.

Anstey Lane,
Newtown Linford,
Leicestershire, May 5th, 1948.

In October of the year 1537 a child was born to the Marquis of Dorset (afterwards created Duke of Suffolk) at his country seat, Bradgate Park in Leicestershire. Although both he and his wife desired a boy, this child and the two that followed were girls. The first of these three children was Lady Jane Grey who became one of the Queens of England, and the other two were the Lady Mary and the Lady Katherine Grey 'Their mother was a niece of Henry the Eighth, and Prince Edward (later King Edward VI, 1547-1553) and Princess Elizabeth (later Queen Elizabeth 1558-1603) were their cousins.

They grew up happily in the beautiful surroundings of Bradgate Park, in spite of the fact that their mother was a sharp tempered woman who did not hesitate to punish them severely upon the least provocation. Lady Katherine was her favourite and was shewn more leniency than the other two, but even she learned to fear that very uncertain temper.

As they grew in stature they became very proficient in the arts and learning of their day, and at the tender age of seven years began to learn to speak Latin and Greek. Lady Jane was the most studious of the three and could often be found in the window seat in the Tower which overlooks the lake and sunken garden, intent upon her studies, when her sisters were romping and playing out of doors. One of their greatest delights was to be allowed to join the Morris Dancers in the Park, and to dance around the May-pole which was erected for the May-day revels each year; but Lady Jane preferred to watch them from her favourite seat in the window.

One day in the year 1545, the sisters were delighted when a message was brought to them by a servant, commanding them to dress as quickly as possible in their very best clothes, and present themselves to their mother in the room which was only used for state occasions; they dressed hurriedly, and in an excited condition proceeded to where they had been directed. They were somewhat in awe of their mother, for she generally sent for them in order to reprimand and punish them; and sometimes was even physically cruel to them, but on this day she was all smiles, and they could hardly believe their own eyes when she brought forward two

Newtown Linford Church showing Memorial Window.

children explaining that they were their cousins, Prince Edward, and Princess Elizabeth, who had come to stay with them for a few days. The young ladies were thrilled by this news, for they saw very few children of their own age. After they had greeted and embraced their new found cousins they were told by their still smiling mother, that they may be excused lessons for the day, and were at liberty to take the cousins down into the park to see the deer and beautiful wild birds which lived there.

Lady Jane and the young prince soon became very firm friends, for they had much in common, both were very keen students of Latin and Greek and in the years that followed they saw a good deal of each other; and often when the young prince was staying at Bradgate they would be found, sitting together in the window seat pouring over some difficult passage in one of the languages they were studying.

The young prince did not enjoy good health, but it was found that he benefited from living in the air of Bradgate, and so on his doctor's advice he went there for a long stay each year; but he could not overcome the malady of the lungs from which he suffered so much pain and discomfort. his helplessness and patience brought forth all the innate tenderness which was the character of Lady Jane and she sorrowed deeply that she could not help him.

As Lady Jane and her sisters grew older they were taken to London each year, where they stayed at Durham House, the family mansion in the Strand. They went to court and met the fashionable people of the day, enjoyed the life of London with its gaiety and pleasure, but were always glad to get back again to their beloved Bradgate, or Brodegate as it was then known.

In due course a Tutor was engaged for them, a Mr. Aylmer, and his patience was often sorely tried by the behaviour of the two younger of the sisters; but of Lady Jane he was very proud, for at the age of fourteen she was said to be, in learning, second only to the royal Princesses. Roger Ascham (Preceptor to the Royal Family) calling on her father one day at Bradgate, and, learning that he was out hunting, asked to be allowed to pay his respects to the young ladies. Lady Jane only was indoors at the

Part of the ruin showing the Tower.

time and as he was led into her presence he noticed that the book she laid down, at his approach, was the Phaedo of Plato in the original Greek. He asked her how, at such a tender age, she could have attained such proficiency, and she answered that she believed it was due to the fact that she had such strict, severe parents, and a very kind and gentle teacher, who taught her with such fair allurements to learning, that it was the only time that brought any real pleasure to her.

She grew to be a very beautiful young lady, and the following description has been given of her: dainty, diminutive, face clear and oval in shape, regular features, placid countenance, rosy smiling lips, a sweet voice, lovely light brown hair and eyes, and a truly grecian nose; of an amiable and sweet tempered disposition. From their earliest years Lady Katherine and Lady Mary had looked up to her as a pattern of virtue and grace, and they loved her very dearly.

By the Spring-time of 1553, the newly made Duke of Northumberland was often to be found at Durham House accompanied by his son, the Lord Guilford Dudley, who invariably sought out Lady Jane. They were quite good friends but had not a great deal in common, for Dudley had very little learning and was not a strong character as subsequent events proved; and Lady Jane and Lord Wardour already entertained warm feelings for each other. The Duchess of Suffolk and the Duke of Northumberland had, however, definite plans for the young couple, and in order to gratify their own selfish ambitions had already decided that they were to marry; but, no one else as yet knew of their plans. The Duchess persistently brought pressure to bear upon the young and tender Lady Jane, and at the end of May, 1553, they were married and went to live at Sion House, the London home of the Northumberlands. The poor girl felt freer and more at peace than she had been before, now that she was away from her overbearing mother; and let it be said for Dudley, he was a kind and considerate husband and she grew to be fond of him, but her new found peace was of short duration and at the end of July it was shattered by the news of the young King's death.

The private chapel of the Greys and part of a ruined Tower.

The delicate Edward VI grew weaker with the years, and at the time of his cousin's marriage was spending the greater part of his time in bed, but he wrote her saying that he would be with her in spirit on her wedding day and that he hoped she would know great happiness in the married state; she little knew then how soon this dear friend of her childhood would pass on to where pain and suffering would be over for him, while her own had still to come. She grieved deeply for him, for the memories she had of the times they had been together at Bradgate were among the very few really happy ones she had known. She had yet to learn how tragic his passing would be for her, what decisions were being made for her or what plans were being formed for the shaping of a destiny over which she would have no control.

On the day following the news of her cousin's death, Lady Jane was awakened early in the morning by unusual sounds below stairs, and on arriving down there, found that her husband was already down and giving audience to her parents the Duke and Duchess of Suffolk, and his father, the Duke of Northumberland, and several other people. When she entered all rose and her father-in-law informed her that she was now Queen. This news was a shock to her, and she, poor girl, could not repress her tears or hide her distress, for at her tender years she did not want the responsibility of the crown; and in her heart she knew that there were others with greater claim. Her mother seeing her distress became very angry, and severely rebuked her, exhorting her to behave in a more Queenly manner; and then went on to tell her that the young King before his death had signed a deed which gave her the right to the crown.

Her husband, noting her unhappy condition, crossed the room and came to her side, and she pleaded with him to save her from being made Queen; but to her surprise he treated her coldly and told her that it was futile to object, he tried to comfort her but she would not be comforted, for she told him, we have been happy together at Sion House, but if I become Queen we shall never know happiness again. He then pleaded with her telling her that it was her duty to accept, and so save the country from the troubles of

Jane refuses to embrace the Roman Faith.

the day. She in turn stated the rights of Mary and Elizabeth, at which her ambitious mother became enraged and standing up and drawing herself up to her full height sternly forbade any further argument on the matter, and her father-in-law, the Duke, handed her a deed which was a copy of the deed of succession, and told her to go to her room and read it carefully, as he required her signature to the original later that day.

Poor Lady Jane, she felt she had no one to whom she could turn for help, for even the husband she had learned to love, and by whom she had believed she was loved, would not help her in this; and after persisting in her refusal for some time, she was ultimately forced to accept that unhappy role, and was proclaimed Queen of England. Several days later Guilford Dudley and Northumberland tried to prevail upon her to put Dudley on the Throne as King, this she refused to do and in consequence a coldness grew up between them and spoiled the affection which had been theirs.

The rascally Northumberland was pleased with himself, for had he not worked very hard to bring this about, by ingratiating himself into the company of the young King, and then, by removing all but his own chosen servants from about him, he persuaded him to bequeath the crown to Jane his cousin, because, he told him, Mary Queen of Scots is excluded by Henry the Eighth's will, and Mary and Elizabeth are illegitimate; they were the daughters of Henry the Eighth and Katherine of Aragon and Anne Boleyn respectively. He also talked to him of Mary's obvious attachment to Popery, and the young King, jealous for the newly formed Protestant faith and fearing for its overthrow if she came to the throne, willingly signed the deed of succession; the two unfortunate young people had indeed become pawns in the game, to transfer still more power to Northumberland.

Jane wore the crown for about ten days, when finding the nation were averse to her succession she willingly returned to a private life happier than she had been since the proclamation. Mary was immediately installed upon the throne with the general approval of the nation.

Some of the Memorial Window Carvings.

Northumberland was put under arrest and on August 22nd, 1553, was executed. The Lady Jane, her husband, and some of their supporters were imprisoned in the Tower. They would probably have escaped with their lives, had not an insurrection been raised in Kent by Sir Thomas Whyat in the hope of recovering the crown for Lady Jane; this was soon quelled however, and the chief promoters of it executed, but it proved fatal to her and her husband, for Mary thenceforth removed every person who in any way might prove dangerous to the throne. She did however offer Lady Jane her life, even then, if she would embrace the Roman faith and she sent important members of that faith to exhort her to become converted; but she would not be persuaded, and told her hearers that she could not change the faith she had held since childhood which meant more than her life to her.

Notice was given to her to prepare for death; a doom which she had expected, and which the experience of her life, and the misfortunes to which she had been subjected, rendered not unwelcome to her. On the day of her execution, February 12th, 1554, her husband asked permission to see her, but she refused her consent, and informed him by messenger that the tenderness of parting would overcome the fortitude of both, and would too much unbend their minds from that constancy which their approaching end demanded of them; their separation she said, would only be for a moment and they would soon rejoin each other in a scene where their affection would be for ever united, and where death, disappointment, and misfortune, could no longer disturb, or have access to their eternal felicity.

Her husband was beheaded first, and she beheld with unshaken firmness, his lifeless body being brought back in a hand cart; she was then herself taken to the scaffold.

She mounted the edifice, and then turned to the watching crowds and addressing them in a speech in which the mildness of her disposition led her to take the blame wholly upon herself, and without uttering any complaint against the severity with which she had been treated, she went forward; with her prayer book in her hand, and praying as she walked. She then knelt down and

FECKHAM'S INTERVIEW WITH LADY JANE GRAY IN THE TOWER

recited the fifty-first psalm, after which her maid, Mistress Tynley, handed her a kerchief to tie about her eyes; turning to the executioner she said, "I pray you dispatch me quickly." He begged her forgiveness for that which he had to do, and she freely forgave; he gently placed her in position, feeling for the block she laid her head upon it, stretched out her body and said, "Lord into thy hands I commend my spirit."

And so died the gentle, learned, Lady Jane, a victim of the ambitions of those who should have been her natural protectors.

Her birth-place is now a ruin, but enough of it still remains to indicate to those who visit the Park some of the beauty of its earlier splendour; there is a legend too about some of the oak trees in the Park which appear to have become stunted in growth and show dead branches at the tops of the trees; It is believed that when the foresters of the day heard of the nature of the death of their beloved Lady Jane, they cried out, "The oak of the forest has fallen, the very trees shall mourn for her." They at once cut out the top-most branches, the leaders of the young oak trees; and whether the legend be true or false, you may see to this day the "Pollarded" oaks in Bradgate Park, a living memorial to the Lady whose greatest pleasure was to study beneath their branches.

In the year 1915, a beautiful stained glass window was placed in the Eastern wall of the church of All Saint's, Newtown Linford, which is situated at the main entrance to the Park; by Mrs. K. H. V. Grey, a descendant of that line of Greys who lived in Bradgate Park for several hundred years, and who still is patron of the church as the Greys have always been. This church would be well known to Lady Jane from her earliest years, and it is fitting that she should at last be commemorated in the sacred building where perhaps were laid the sure foundations of that pious resignation which gave to her tragedy an almost sacramental character. Perhaps it was in Newtown Linford Church that there first came to her the secret of the quiet self possession that sustained her in the last dread moments of her life.

The window which is above the altar is inscribed "To the glory of God and in memory of Lady Jane Grey, born 1537, beheaded 1554" and "The pure in heart shall see God." The panelling round the altar bears many direct reminders of Lady Jane, that on the North wall is inscribed with the words "Thou shalt make me hear of joy and gladness," from the fifty-first psalm which she read in the English version while waiting to be led to the scaffold. On the South side is her last prayer"Lord into Thy hands I commend my spirit." On the North end of the East wall is "In Memoriam," and on the South end of the same wall is "Jane the Quene" the spelling is a copy of her signature to a document preserved in the British Museum. North and South of the retable are panels bearing the crowned monogram "J.G." The golden crown is fewelled silver and blue, the metals and colour of the Grey Arms-Barry of 6 argent and azure; below are a York and Lancaster rose, the claim to the throne that was advanced on her behalf having been based on her descent from both houses. The promise of a young girl's life is symbolised by the Spring blossoms, the may alternating with the rose and the vine and the ripe golden corn edging the shelf of the retable.

Printed by
GARNER PRESS CO. LTD.,
HAVELOCK STREET,
LEICESTER.

Appendix E

Letters

9 Northcote Rd
Southsea
10.30 am.
7/9/29.

Dearest.

I hope you have received my letter by now & that you are all right. Southsea is a beautiful place & it is full of people. I have never seen so many young people at a place before. the place seems crowded with young girls. We have just taken tickets for a boat trip out to the Course, we start at 11.45, so we should be on the sea a good time today, as the race is expected to last until about 4.30. The Daily Mail is broadcasting music as we sit here on the pier waiting for the boat to come in. We had a very nice sea trip round the forts & Italian Warships last night. We were out about $1\frac{1}{2}$ hours & it was very nice. There are some very nice liners & yachts out here anchored to see the race.

later. It was a splendid race, & we got within 500 yards of Ryde Pier head, where they start & finish. As you will have seen by the papers England won with a speed of 328 miles an hour. You cannot imagine the deafening roar as they passed over our heads at 350 miles an hour. This is a lovely place, I do wish you were here, there is endless to see & it is a splendid starting place for lots of visits & trips. I hope you have had a good day, & that the children are enjoying themselves. As we shall be leaving here early on Tuesday morning, I wouldn't address any letters to here after you get this (which I hope will be first post on Monday.) It is just a week come tomorrow since I left you & it seems at least a month. I hope the next 6 days doesn't seem as

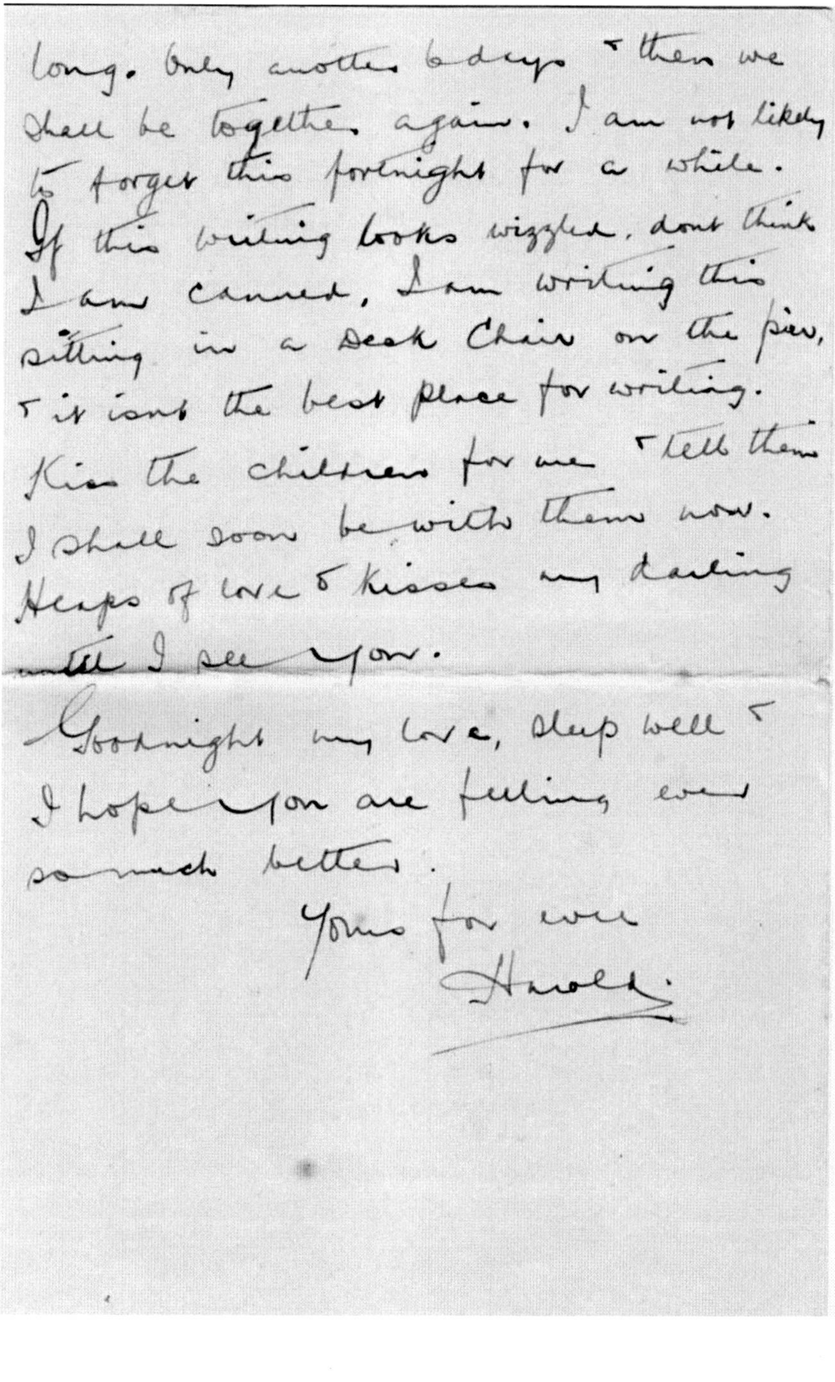
long. Only another 6 days & then we
shall be together again. I am not likely
to forget this fortnight for a while.
If this writing looks wizzled, dont think
I am canned, I am writing this
sitting in a Deck Chair on the pier,
& it isnt the best place for writing.
Kiss the children for me & tell them
I shall soon be with them now.
Heaps of love & kisses my darling
until I see you.

Goodnight my love, sleep well &
I hope you are feeling ever
so much better.

Yours for ever

Harold.

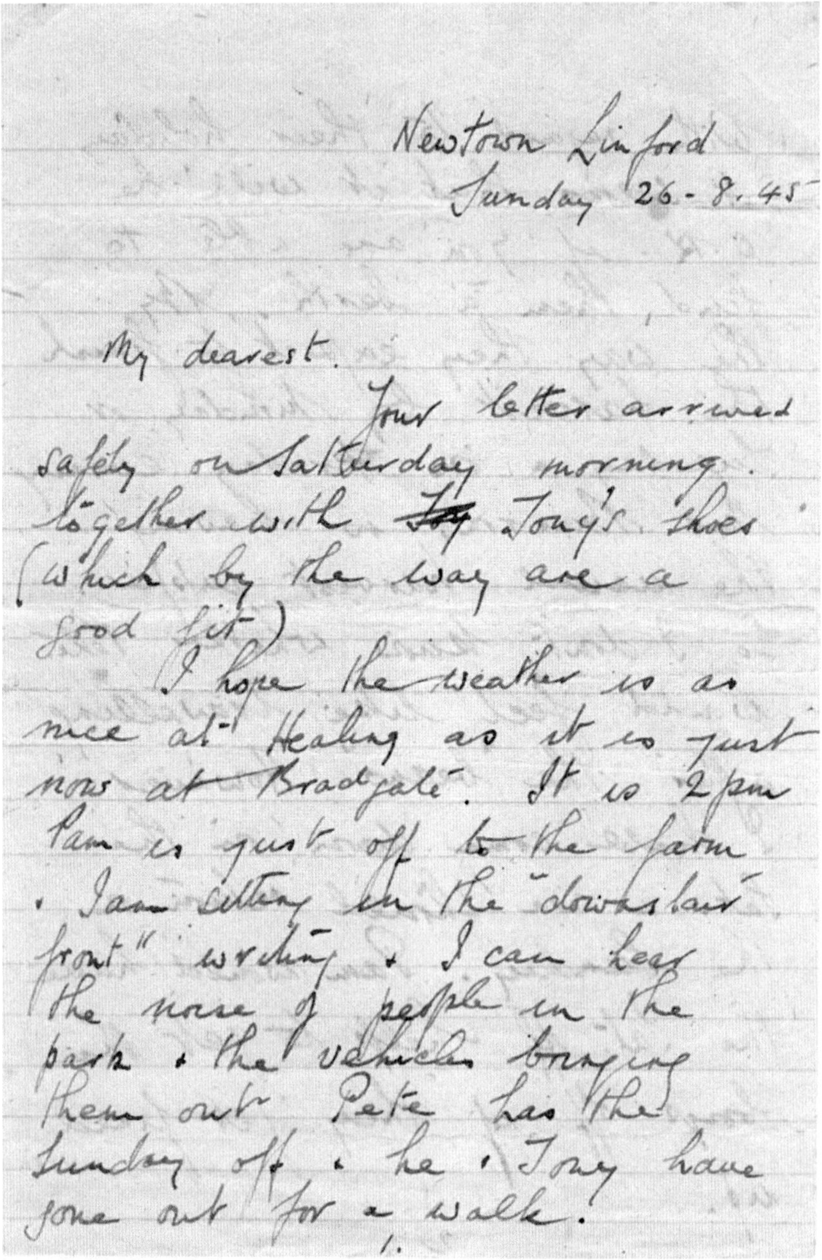

Newtown Linford
Sunday 26-8-45

My dearest.

Your letter arrived safely on Saturday morning. together with Tony's shoes (which by the way are a good fit)

I hope the weather is as nice at Healing as it is just now at Bradgate. It is 2pm Pam is just off to the farm & I am sitting in the "downstairs front" writing & I can hear the noise of people in the park & the vehicles bringing them out. Pete has the Sunday off & he & Tony have gone out for a walk.

With regard to their holiday it seems that it will be O.K. if you are able to find them a berth. By the way they expect to finish the harvest by Monday or Tuesday & on Friday evening Mr Burrows is having the usual harvest supper. So I don't know whether Pete would feel like travelling after the "beano". However I shall come down on the Sat. & we should return on the Sunday. Pam would have the Sat. off & help to get the boys off if they get fixed up.

2

This week end we had Joan over came Sat. evening & will return 5.30 this evening. She & Pam did cleaning & cooking to-day. So we found her helpful.

I thought of you & I on Friday celebrating behind a glass of gin & lime but it turned out to be only wishful thinking. You say you are missing me very much, I bet you are not missing me half as much as I am you. My sole consolation is the fact that it is for the benefit of your health so must not be impatient. When you come back better in health & rested that will be the best reward for a lonely husband like yours truly.

Pam went to get her land army clothes during her day off on Fri. She bought a pair of socks for my birthday. Elva sent me a card & enclosed some letters from Colin which I am sending to you. I enclose also a cutting from the 'Mirror' which I think faithfully depicts the clothes outlook for the next few months "never mind eh".

I hope you received my last two letters which I sent to you on Wednesday & Friday morning respectively.

Well how is the fish trade? have associated tasty fish meals with you when my mind

4

frequently wanders into thoughts of you & what you may be doing. I expect by now you will have acquired that atmosphere of "retiredness" typical of Healingites. Slow lazy & comfortable, really just what you want, expect also you will return with a trace of dialect savouring of the "north". I am so sorry to learn that you still have the pain I do so hope that by now it has disappeared & that the next week will prove to be a painless one & ~~also~~ with a feeling of returning strength.

You mention Sam & Pete getting wet. No, last week they managed to keep dry in spite of odd showers.

5

To-night I shall go to church & let Mr Bland know about 'time' off next Sunday for someone to take my turn. I shall think of you whilst I am there & missing you from by my side.

What do you think of the sudden lifting of lease & lend? I trust that some other system will take its place with similar benefits to tide us over the next 12 months.

Well I am closing so that Joan can post this letter before 4.30.

Keeping smiling through my darling - heaps of affectionate thoughts & a parting kiss with all my love from your sweetheart.

Cyril

Bibliography

Alcock N.W, Hughes M (2008) Atherstone: A Pleasantly Placed Town, Phillmore and Co Ltd, Chichester publishers

Amos Dr D. (2012) Infant Mortality in three East Midland towns: similarities and difference http://eastmidlandshistory.org.u/

Amos Dr D. (2012) 'It is on the lives of infants that unhealthy influences have their deadliest effects': Combating infant mortality in Nottingham and Leicester 1890-1910. www.nottsheritagegateway.org.uk

Beckett J. (2006) Leicester Becomes a City 1919 in Transactions of the Leicestershire Archaeological and History Society, Vol. 80, p. 151-162

Davies P.D.O (1999) Multi-Drug Resistant Tuberculosis, Priory Journals, Priory Lodge Education Ltd, 1999, http://www.priory.com

Dirveiks L, Vero J. Information Board in Aldi Car Park, Atherstone, produced by Dirveiks and Vero, Atherstone Civic Society and Friends of Atherstone Heritage and supported by Aldi

Faber and Faber Ltd, publishers, License to print passages from 'The Four Quartets', 'Burnt Norton', and 'Little Gidding' by TS Eliot, granted by kind permission.

Friends of Atherstone Heritage (2012) The Yards of Atherstone, printed by Anchor Print Group Ltd, Syston.

History of War, dates of the Menin Road Ridge and Third Battle of Ypres www.historyofwar.org

Johnson B. (2007) Images of Eingland, 100 years of Leicester Cinema, The History Press

Journeyman (2006) in Harris (Ed), Dictionary of architecture and construction. New York, NY: McGraw-Hill in https://en.wikipedia.org/wiki/Journeyman

Liddle P. (2013) Ed, Passchendaele in Perspective: The Third Battle of Ypres, Pen and Sword Military, Pen and Sword pubs.

Old Ordnance Survey Maps (2002) Leicester (NW) 1902, Leicestershire Sheet 31.10, 2nd Edition 1904, The Godfrey Edition, www.alangodfreymaps.co.uk

Pamphilon E.M. (1948) Lady Jane Grey of Bradgate Park, 5th May 1948, Garner Press Co Ltd, Havelock Street, Leicester

Pamphilon E.M. (1971) The sad, true story of a gypsy princess, Leicester Mercury, Friday July 16th 1971

Pamphilon E.M. (1948) The Good Old Days? Past and Present, The Socialist Leader, Saturday April 17th 1948 p.8

Record Office for Leicestershire, Leicester and Rutland, Wigston, Burial information, for Frank and Doris Hartell Welford Road Cemetery, Leicester.

Record Office for Leicestershire, Leicester and Rutland, Wigston. Record 2D74/5 Desford Boys School Admissions Register.

REID A. (2005) The Effects of the 1918-1919 Influenza Pandemic on Infant and Child Health in Derbyshire. *Medical History. 2005; 49 (1) 29-54*

Stevens S. (2014) Heritage can be the glue that binds together a community, *Newfoundpool News, Keeping our community connected (Christmas 2014) pp10-11www.dmu.ac.uk/documents/technology-documents/undergraduate-courses/journalism/newfoundpool-community-news.pdf,* citing information from a personal interview with Professor John Martin, Professor of Agrarian History, De Montfort University, Leicester. The interview was undertaken by John Dilley's journalism group, De Montfort University.

The Newtown Linford Church Magazine, ISSUE NUMBER 90 December 2011/January 2012

Web:UK, Coal Mining Accidents and Deaths Index 1700-1950 [database on-line] Provo, UT, USA: Ancestry.com Operations, inc., 2013

Warwickshire County Records Office, photographs of Atherstone and Avins Yard, Collections PHN213/3, PHN 213/25, PHN213/37

1917 Total war in Flanders, Visitors Guide 3.6.2017-31.12.2017

www.ancestry.co.uk/uk1901census

www.ancestry.co.uk/uk1911census

www.british-history.ac.uk/leics/vol4/pp447-456

www.markfieldhistory.btck.couk/MarkfieldHospital

www.nationalarchives.gov.uk.

www.vocabulary.com/apoplexy

Acknowledgements

Alma Tingay, for providing clarification and information about her mother Ethel Martin.

Anthony Hartell (Uncle Tony) for his help and encouragement, identifying photographs and dredging up memories and information, and generally helping to fit together some pieces of the family jigsaw puzzles.

Bryan Prytherch, my husband who has never complained about my many hours spent on the computer, and accommodating as always, trawled with me around Southport in search of Harold's convalescent home, accompanied me to Desford Boys School for the Remembrance Service to honour great uncle George and to Ypres, Belgium to find George's memorial in Tyne Cot. As always, he has been my support and my rock.

Carol Hartell my mum who sadly passed away in May 2015. She and I spent precious hours trying to decipher and understand some of Harold and Cyril's letters, language and handwriting. Being a generation removed she found this much easier than I, and her input is a treasured memory.

Christine Freeman (Jenking) for kind permission to use the Michael Chetwynd mural of the Atherstone Ball Game in the book.

Christine Uzzel, Elsie's granddaughter, thank you for not pushing the 'letters' into a drawer where they may never have seen the light of day again for further untold decades.

Claire Donovan, Initial Contact and Assessment Manager Helpline@meningitisnow.org for providing information and insight about meningitis and 'meningitis TB' and giving permission for her quote to be used.

Dr John Sutton, Royal Leicestershire Regiment Researcher for accessing information about George, Harold's brother and his military history.

Friends of Welford Road Cemetery, Leicester, particularly Ian Sainthouse and Jackie Marsh for information about Doris and Frank Hartell and Sarah Martin.

Hazel Allen and Jim Martin, (Evelyn and Henry Martin's grandchildren) for their assistance in discovering more about Elsie, Emma and Ethel, the other Martin children, and Evelyn Aldwinkle. Also thank you both for connecting me with so many lovely relatives.

Hazel Allen for sharing her wonderful family tree website and giving permission to use information from it in this publication.

Harry Aldwinkle, who provided the link with Hazel Allen, and Jim Martin.

Ian Vickers, and Pauline Pettitt from the 'Ibstock Historical Society'. Their advice, encouragement and help in solving our family tree puzzles have been very much appreciated. Facebook web page www.facebook.com/groups

Iris Gleeson for the last minute newspaper article giving further insight into the name of Pamphilon and Elsie's WI involvement.

Jackie Harris, Elsie's granddaughter for proof reading the letters, and giving guidance on grammar and punctuation and being a great encouragement during the process, along with 'Uncle Tony' her father.

Janet Scrivens local author of 'The Late Elephant, and 'A House in Rutland' for proof reading, and for her enthusiasm and encouragement.

Jeanette and Barrie McNeil for their hospitality and kindness on a very special day in April 2016 quote.... *"We have loved living in this house and now we know why. It was built and lived in - in those early years - with such love and determination. How I would have loved to meet Elsie May"*

John and Celia Parton of the Nuneaton and North Warwickshire Family History Society, for the tour of Atherstone, and for the photographs of Avins Yard.

Leicester Co-operative Society who hold copyright for the letterhead on which two of Harold's letters are written.

Linda Storer, Elsie's granddaughter who helped to decipher some of the letters, shared her memories of Thornton, some of which I had long forgotten until she brought them to light again, for accompanying me on fact finding expeditions and for proof reading.

Lynda Mackness for her help in finding information about Evelyn, Harold's sister.

Margaret Brant, and Margaret Abbott for their help in finding additional information about Edith, Harold's sister and for Edith's photograph.

Markfield Historical Society for their kind permission to print anything from their site which would be useful
www.markfieldhistory.btck.couk/MarkfieldHospital

Muriel Walker for sharing her memories of Mrs. Pam and the Women's Institute

Nigel and Marianne Lane for their memories of Elsie and Thornton

Pete Harris for his expertise and time spent in improving the photographs, thank you, much appreciated, a job well done, 'because we're worth it!'

Peter Hartell and his son Andy for providing information about Walter, Harold's younger brother.

Shirley Raithby and Alison Sadler, Emma's daughter and granddaughter, for sharing their extensive family tree research, particularly regarding Emma Martin and giving permission for it to be used in this publication.

Timothy Hartell, Elsie's grandson for the photographs of the 'Roll Top Desk' where the journey started, for his company on a voyage of discovery to 'The Desford Boys School' and for helping to fit together another piece of the family puzzle through the Desford Boys School 'Old Boys 2014 Remembrance Service' on YouTube. Also for his skill and assistance in putting together the photograph on the front cover.

The 'Old Boys Network' of The Desford Boys School for sharing information from their research into the history of the School and for giving permission for it to be used in this publication.

Every effort has been made to appropriately and extensively reference and acknowledge the source of all the information used for this publication. If anyone or anything has been missed I offer my sincere apologies.

Contact details: sal.cherith@ntlworld.com

Opinions expressed in the letters are those of the original authors reflecting the views and thinking of that particular era.

The compilation of this book is a 'not for profit' venture. Any eventual proceeds after expenses will benefit three charities:

Mary's Meals
Ibstock Historical Society
The Bradgate Park Trust

If you have enjoyed even parts of this book, you may also enjoy 'Tales from Old Swepi' two local historical novels by author Janet Scrivens:

The Late Elephant

In 1891 Ada Elverson, a fourteen year old lives with her family at The Late Elephant coaching inn on the outskirts of Swepstone in Leicestershire. The whole village attend her sister's wedding day at St Peter's Church returning to the Inn for a day of revelry. A week later Ada is travelling by steam train to take up an apprenticeship as a cook with the Ludlam family at Glenfield Mill. Her new life holds some shocking challenges.

A House in Rutland

In 1901 Ada leaves the sleepy village of Swepstone for the second time to take up a position as a cook in a country mansion known as Burley on the Hill in charge of a team of servants. The owner, Mr George Finch is a direct descendant of The Earls of Nottingham and resides there with his wife and six daughters. Mr Neville, a handsome steward, takes a fancy to Ada while Miss Christina, a ladies maid takes her in hand and introduces her to a new and exciting lifestyle full to bursting with fashion, travel and pleasure; not all of which gains Ada's approval.